THE BLACK FAMILY

The Church's Role in the African American Community

C. ANTHONY HUNT

THE BLACK FAMILY
The Church's Role in the African American Community

The Rhodes-Fulbright Library

by C. Anthony Hunt

ProdCode: CSS/250/2.85/165/20

Library of Congress
Catalog in Publication

00-103318

International Standard Book Number

1-55605-305-3

Copyright © 2000 by C. Anthony Hunt

ALL RIGHTS RESERVED

Printed in the United States of America

Wyndham Hall Press
Bristol, IN 46507-9460

TABLE OF CONTENTS

INTRODUCTION i

PART I
THEOLOGICAL AND SOCIO-CULTURAL ANALYSIS

CHAPTER ONE
  A THEOLOGICAL FRAMEWORK 1

CONTEMPORARY ISSUES FACING THE AFRICAN
AMERICAN CHURCH AND FAMILY 11

CHAPTER TWO
  AIDS: THE DEADLY ENEMY 12

CHAPTER THREE
  POVERTY: THE EFFECTS OF ECONOMIC INJUSTICE ON
  AFRICAN AMERICAN FAMILIES 21

CHAPTER FOUR
  ADDICTION: SUBSTANCE ABUSE AND AFRICAN AMERICAN FAMILIES 26

PART II
PRINCIPLES FOR THE CHURCH'S ROLE IN AFRICAN AMERICAN FAMILY PRESERVATION

CHAPTER FIVE
  PRINCIPLE ONE - UNITY 37

CHAPTER SIX
  PRINCIPLE TWO - HOLINESS 40

CHAPTER SEVEN
  PRINCIPLE THREE - CATHOLICITY 43

CHAPTER EIGHT
   PRINCIPLE FOUR - APOSTOLICITY 46

CHAPTER NINE
   PRINCIPLE FIVE - KERYGMA (PROCLAMA-
   TION/WORSHIP) 50

CHAPTER TEN
   PRINCIPLE SIX - DIAKONIA (SERVICE) 58

CHAPTER ELEVEN
   PRINCIPLE SEVEN - KOINONIA (FELLOWSHIP) 61

CONCLUSION 65

APPENDIX 1
   QUALITY OF LIFE RETREATS: A Model for
   Ministry with Aids Sufferers 67

APPENDIX 2
   CHRISTIANS IN RECOVERY: A Model for Church-
   based Addiction Ministry 71

APPENDIX 3
   THE AMES UNITED METHODIST CHURCH
   BROCHURE OF MINISTRIES INCLUDING
   VISION STATEMENT 77

APPENDIX 4
   THE PRINCIPLES FOR THE CHURCH'S ROLE
   IN AFRICAN AMERICAN FAMILY PRESERVA-
   TION - SUCCINCTLY STATED 81

BIBLIOGRAPHY 85

ABOUT THE AUTHOR 93

INTRODUCTION

Over the course of history, the black church has played a significant role in the development and preservation of African American families. Despite the tremendous difficulties experienced as a result of slavery and the racism that has heretofore plagued American society, the black church and family remain, by virtually all accounts, the two most enduring institutions in African American life. The black church and family have been seen as a union that is indelibly linked, with the life of either inextricably dependent upon the strength of the other.

As in the past, the future vitality and preservation of African American family life depends largely upon how churches wholistically address the needs that exist within the family context.

African American family preservation involves the appropriation of those spiritual and temporal resources including values, traditions, methods, processes, systems, philosophies, and theologies which will result in the ongoing sustainment, vitality and valuation of family structures and communities.

In many respects, this analysis is a culmination of more than eighteen years of study undertaken in the disciplines of Theology, Economics, Business, and Technology at various institutions of higher learning including the University of Maryland, Troy State University, Wesley Theological Seminary, The Graduate Theological Foundation, and St. Mary's Seminary and University.

My objective and perspective has been one of perpetually seeking to arrive at a practical and coherent Biblical theology for the life of the Christian church. I strive to articulate ways in which the church in this contemporary age might more faithfully and fervently engage in transforming the society in which we live while spreading Scriptural holiness.

In completing this study on the black church's role in strengthening and preserving African American families, it is my prayer that God will make me sufficient for the task that has been set before me.

PURPOSE/THESIS

In the continuing quest to comprehend the role and mission of the black church as we move into the twenty-first century, it is clear that the church stands at a cross-roads grappling with what will be its direction and focus for the future. A portion of this dilemma will be addressed - specifically - the church's role in the context of contemporary African American family life. While, the black church has traditionally been one of the most stable institutions in African American communities - today it experiences some difficulty in clearly defining its role and mission. In part, this might be the result of the struggles out of which the black church was borne - many of which continue to adversely affect African American individuals, families and communities.

These struggles have included the atrocities and death experienced by many Africans during the middle passage, the brutality and dehumanizing experiences of slavery, the evil and injustice of Jim Crow and other manifestations of individual and institutional racism, as well as the unfairness, inequality and deprivation of the related abject poverty that continues to plague many African American families and communities today. It is important to note that historically, the black church has existed within the context of each of these realities, while perpetually attempting to define and redefine itself as it seeks to be relevant given changing societal realities.

This project offers a practical framework for the black church's engagement in the task of African American family preservation. The primary objective is to develop a model that can be used by churches to support the critical needs of African American families.

One critical assumption made throughout is that any analysis of African American ecclesiology is fundamentally a study of a segment of the larger Body of Christ. The black church has never stood as a body in and of itself, but is a part of the church universal. Although borne out of the particular context of African American life and culture, the black church is essentially a manifestation of God's overall divine mission (missio dei). Certainly, there is but one Lord, one faith, and one baptism (Ephesians 4:5). Therefore, African American ecclesiology is to be understood within the broader contexts of both American ecclesiology and African traditional religions and cultures - which certainly have immensely impacted African American religious life.

METHODOLOGY

The overall epistomological concern involves ways in which one obtains and rationalizes knowledge about the contemporary church's role in African American family preservation. Theological perspectives of the black church and the African American family will be explored by drawing upon faith resources from both the past and present.

Throughout, there will be references to various theological perspectives which have in the past, and continue to emerge within African American communities. These include various forms of what has commonly been termed black theology, liberation theology, neo-pentecostalism, and neo-evangelicalism. The objective is to ascertain - beyond any particular denominational distinctive or theological strand - the effects of these and other theologies upon the black church and family.

In addition to the usage of theology, the integrative methodology employed will involve the use of sociology, anthropology, philosophy, history, literature, among other disciplines.

Historical analysis of black churches and families will help us to see that, in contemporary context, form and practice, the black church has several direct ecclesial forbearers. Social analysis, both in historical and contemporary context, helps us to focus upon some of the environmental, communal, political and economic factors which have led the black church to the position that it now occupies in American religiosity and culture.

Peter Paris, in *The Social Teaching of the Black Churches*, suggests that the black churches, under the norm of the black Christian tradition, are characterized by their common quest for human freedom and justice - that is the equality of all persons under God.[1]

This quest for freedom and justice - germane to the black church's very being - will be a principle that underlies much of what is discussed throughout.

As a matter of praxis, the seven principles that will be developed as the foundation of the model for the black church's role in African American family preservation are informed by several extant sources. These include: (1) A study of the history and sociology of black churches and families in America; (2) A lifetime of personal involvement and investment in the life of black churches and family life; (3) Interviews and discussions with church, academic and community leaders from throughout the United States regarding past and future perspectives on the church's role in African American family preservation; and (4) Pastoral ministry in three United Methodist Congregations where members have been predominantly African American.

In each of these ministry settings, we engaged in the intentional process of developing and applying principles with expectations of strengthening congregational life and families. The goal was the achievement of demonstrable improvements in the quality of family life of church and community members. This was especially evident at Ames United Methodist Church in Bel Air, Maryland, where I served as pastor from 1992 until the summer of 1998. This project is essentially a reflection of the learnings from this ministerial setting.

I currently serve in ministry as the Executive Director of the United Methodist Church's Multi-Ethnic Center for Ministry, where one of the primary objectives is to develop programs and provide resources and consultation to racial ethnic congregations and ministries which are seeking to become more vital in their witness to Christ.

It is my experience that a focus on the church as the family of God is critical to strengthening all faith communities - especially African American congregations. The construct of the family of God has roots in traditional African tribal life where the valuation of family was consistently affirmed and is exemplified in the often repeated Yoruba proverb that says "it takes a village to raise a child."

In Part I of this project, theological and socio-cultural analysis will be provided in light of the historical and contemporary relationship of the black church and family. The principles in Part II are derived from two primary sources: (1) The four classical "marks" of the Christian church as enumerated in the Nicene Creed (325 A.D.); and (2) Theologian Dorothee

Solle's thesis regarding the essential elements of the authentic Christian church.[2]

These principles serve as the foundation of the model for the church's role in African American family preservation:

(1) Unity
(2) Holiness
(3) Catholicity (Universality)
(4) Apostolicity
(5) Kerygma (Proclamation)
(6) Diakonia (Service)
(7) Koinonia (Fellowship)

It is expected that this model could be used as a tool to help churches: (1) better understand the critical importance and nature of the family of God, (2) better comprehend the historical and contemporary connections between the church and African American families, and (3) develop ministries which will positively impact families within the context of the vitality and growth of African American congregations in the future.

Various terms will be used when speaking of the African American people and church. These will include "Negro", "Black", and "African American". Usage depends largely on the historical context being addressed. Thus, "Negro" might typically refer to earlier historical periods (e.g. the slave period and reconstruction); "Black" might generally refer to more recent historical periods (e.g. the Civil Rights movement, Black Power, and Black Theology); and "African American" generally pertains to the period from the mid-1980's to the present.

Any overlaps in the usage of these terms are due to: (1) the continued usage of each in some circles even today, and (2) the fact that it has not always been definitively clear - there is no clear consensus - as to when a certain term came into greater usage than its predecessor. Essentially, each term speaks of the same people - those who are direct descendants of persons brought to America from the African shores - mostly as slaves.

A BRIEF PROFILE OF AMES UNITED METHODIST CHURCH

Ames United Methodist Church was founded in 1885 as a community of Negro Christians who sensed the need to meet for fellowship and worship in the town of Bel Air, Maryland. The church immediately affiliated with the Methodist Episcopal denomination, and has had a rather stable existence over the last 113 years.

Ames Church has remained steeped in its traditions over the years. I believe this has served both to help and hinder the church's vitality and witness. Like many mainline churches in the Central Maryland region, Ames has experienced membership declines in the past, and has not always engaged in wholistic ministry with its membership and the broader community.

Bel Air is a town with a population of about 5,000 people that sits in the center of Harford County - located about 30 miles north of Baltimore, Maryland and 65 miles south of Philadelphia, Pennsylvania. Formerly a rural community, and now a suburb of Baltimore - Bel Air is currently experiencing above normal population growth due primarily to significant increases in residential and industrial development over the past ten years.

Ames Church has been a beneficiary of this regional growth, having experienced more than 50% growth in membership since 1992, from 188 members to more than 275 members currently. Over the same period, the church has experienced significant growth in its budget (from less than $60,000 to more than $150,000), and expansion of programs where it has become what church growth consultant and author Lyle Schaller refers to as a "seven-day-a-week" church.[3]

The church's ministry has become more regional in scope, as it is now called to deal with the changing demographics of surrounding communities. Ames Church has become known for its outreach ministries with low income, and drug addicted persons, along with other individuals and families experiencing social dislocation and marginalization. It is projected that the church's membership will exceed 400 members by the year 2005.

As it seeks to respond to the changes in its midst, and address the needs and interests of newer, younger members and families, the church is challenged by the traditions, practices and attitudes that have served to hinder vitality and growth in the past. As pastor, I sought to provide leadership in managing this transition on two levels.

First, a task force was commissioned in early 1993 that was named the "Vision Committee." The task of the Vision Committee was to study, analyze and discern the missional needs of the church as it moved toward the 21st century. The question that remained before the Vision Committee was "What is God calling the church to be, as it moves into the future?" The objectives were to (1) develop the church's vision statement, and (2) devise the strategic plan sufficient to implement the vision statement. One critical missional concern that the Vision Committee had to address in developing the strategic plan was the current condition of the physical plant.

The church's current building was constructed in 1915, and is 83 years old. Essentially, it is a five room structure with a sanctuary that seats approximately 200 people, with a fellowship hall that was built in 1984 and serves multiple purposes as an educational and meeting facility. Additionally, the parsonage - located on church property - has been converted to office, educational and meeting space to address the interim needs for additional space in which to do ministry.

Given the projected growth of the church and community, and the incumbent needs for more space, the Ames Vision Committee recommended in July 1994 that the church construct a new worship facility - to include a family life center - on a larger piece of property. This recommendation was unanimously adopted, and Ames Church is presently engaged in a major capital fund-raising campaign and is searching for the land upon which to construct the new facility. The projected cost for the building project is $1.5 million.[4]

Secondly, I sought to lead the congregation in addressing the transitional needs of the church and community through the development and implementation of various principles of family preservation, with the expectation of increasing the church's overall vitality. In focusing on the various forms and manifestations of African American family life among us - and affirming our call to be the family of God - the church remained in constant prayer and evaluation about the manner in which every aspect of ministry was being performed. This resulted in the church's plans and programs becoming focused on God's call for us to reach and preserve families.

Ministries were intentionally designed to provide pastoral care, nurture and education to members and the broader community. Our worship experiences, Bible studies and times of fellowship were some of the major ministries where this re-emphasis on family life became increasingly evident.

We began the process of appropriating and externalizing what it meant to be the family of God. In the intentional implementation of principles which affirmed, developed and preserved African American families, we began to witness God's work in our midst. The church began to come together and to grow in ways that it had not experienced in its recent past.

§ § §

ENDNOTES

1. Peter Paris, *The Social Teaching of the Black Churches* (Philadelphia, PA: Fortress Press, 1985), p. 15.

2. Dorothee Solle, *Thinking About God: An Introduction to Theology* (Philadelphia: Trinity Press International, 1990), p. 141.

3. Lyle Schaller, *The Seven Day-A-Week Church* (Nashville: Abingdon Press, 1992), Schaller offers characteristics of the "seven-day-a-week church throughout the book.

4. Detailed findings from this and three other African-American new church projects are included in *Building Hope: New Church Development in the African-American Community* (New York: General Board of Global Ministries, 1997). I was one of three co-authors of this work.

PART ONE

THEOLOGICAL AND SOCIO-CULTURAL ANALYSIS

CHAPTER ONE

A THEOLOGICAL FRAMEWORK

The theological task of African American churches involves wholistically addressing the moral and social matters which affect black families and communities. This is accomplished through the continued discovery and cultivation of those spiritual, human, relational and material resources which have served to sustain the church over time. It is helpful to begin any study of the church with an analysis of the sources that can serve as the church's theological foundation.

The integration of Scripture, tradition, experience and reason into what was termed, by United Methodist historical theologian Albert Outler, the "Wesley Quadrilateral" offers a balanced approach in which the church might more clearly and profoundly comprehend how it is called to live out its faith.[1] Such an analysis helps in understanding the past, present and future relationship of the African American church and family, and the prospects for the preservation and vitality of both.

SCRIPTURE

African-Americans have generally viewed the Bible as a source of unquestionable strength and wisdom, and as the essential foundation of spiritual and social values. According to Cain Hope Felder, author of *Troubling Biblical Waters: Race, Class and Family*, it is well-known that the Bible has come to occupy a central place in the religions of the black diaspora. Biblical stories, themes, personalities, and images have inspired, captivated, given meaning, and served as a basis of hope for a liberated and enhanced material life.[2]

The New Testament has a distinct concern for greater priority on quality relationships in the household (Greek:oikos/okia), which emerges as a theological paradigm for membership in the Household of God.[3]

Felder sees a particular theological challenge and opportunity to make the biblical story relevant, given the contemporary realities of the black family. The task of the Bible scholar is to examine and determine what the Bible.

as a foundational document of the Church, says, particularly in light of its ancient context. The task of the Bible scholar becomes hermeneutics when he or she attempts to determine the text's meaning and relevance today. Here the exegete must learn from the theologian, even as the Black Church enters into a new dialogue with both. There is much to learn from recent developments in liberation theology ... All liberation theologies agree that one's own group's experience is a legitimate context for establishing categories and criteria for theological dialogue and a mode of extracting from and identifying with the theological process evident in the Bible.[4]

To learn from the liberation theologians is for the Black Church to develop a new respect for and appreciation of the hurts, needs, and hopes of black families and households as loci for "doing theology."[5]

The black church, in its contemporary context, faces the significant task of reappropriating ancient Bible stories and themes in ways that are relevant to the present realities of African-American families. This involves tapping the deep streams of past Biblical understanding, while building upon these past understandings in ways that help in the development of a hermeneutic that intentionally promotes the wholistic preservation and perpetual progress of African American families and communities in contemporary society.

TRADITION

In order to fully comprehend the current conditions prevalent in African American families and communities, it is important to place the realities of black family and church life into some historical context. Here it is essential to recognize the oppressive nature of slavery in America.

Historians such as John Hope Franklin in *From Slavery to Freedom*, have recounted in graphic detail many of the atrocities faced by African peoples as they were brought to the American shores as slaves. As the first known Africans arrived in the New World at Jamestown in 1619, there began a systematic process of dehumanization of persons and disintegration of families and community. The social and emotional effects of this is evidenced in that family units were typically physically separated. The obvious psychological effects of this social dislocation involved persons being viewed and treated as less than human beings.[6]

These early slave experiences were in stark contrast to most African cultures which affirmed and rewarded human attributes such as strength, valor, courage, trustworthiness and family.

The enslavement of the Negro not only destroyed the traditional African system of kinship and other forms of organized social life but it made insecure and precarious the most elementary form of social life which tended to sprout anew, so to speak, on American soil - the family. There was, of course, no legal marriage and the relation of the husband and father to his wife and children was a temporary relationship dependent upon the will of the white masters and the exigencies of the plantation regime. Although it was necessary to show some regard for the biological tie between slave mother and her offspring, even their relationship was not always respected by the masters. Nevertheless, under the most favorable conditions of slavery, as for example, among the privileged skilled artisans and the favored house servants, some stability in family relations and a feeling of solidarity among the members of the slave households did develop. This, in fact, represented the maximum social cohesion that was permitted to exist among the transplanted Negroes.[7]

Wallace Charles Smith, in *The Church in the Life of the Black Family*, points out that many studies have come out recently which deal with the rising trends of brokenness experienced by the black family. The problem with these studies, according to Smith, is that they have not taken into account the critical importance of understanding the history and role of the church in its relationship to the black family.[8]

It was out of the experience of slavery that the black church was born. The Christian church formed the basis of social cohesion among blacks amidst the discontinuities of American slave culture. As they evolved in black communities, churches served as socially conscious institutions which were not solely concerned with religious matters. The church as an institution sought to address the various societal concerns facing families and the broader community.

In 1921, Carter G. Woodson chronicled in *The History of the Negro Church* the vital role of the black church - largely Methodists and Baptists - in effecting positive change upon the social, political and economic life of black communities in the years immediately following slavery.[9]

Peter Paris, in *The Social Teaching of the Black Churches*, suggests that, like John Wesley and Martin Luther King, and many other social activists within the church over history, there is no indication that Negro Churches were formed merely to start new churches, but these churches derived out of the needs of the community.[10]

The Negro Church arose out of the socio-political context that involved factors such as racism, the disparate poverty and deprivation among Negroes, inordinate family distress, and the resultant dysfunction.

Thus, there has historically been an indelible link between African American families and the black church. The church and the family have been the most visible, and typically, the most stable institutions in the black community. J. Deotis Roberts, in *Roots of a Black Future* shares:

> We have studied the history and sociology of the black family and have allowed our doctrine of the church in the black traditions to emerge out of this context. The extended family has been employed as a way of imaging the black family. Since our goal has been to make these two primary black institutions mutually supportive, it has been proper to family image to reference ecclesiology ... Since black families are the source of the black church's life and growth, the measure of its ministry to black families will determine the quality of its own mission.[11]

Roberts focuses on the notion of the black family as "ecclesiola", little church. It has been one of the progenitors of faith, and an instrument of engagement with the black church as an institution. The reclamation and reappropriation of the link of black family and church will be critical to the ongoing strengthening of African American communities in the future.

The extended nature of the black family is perhaps the clearest manifestation of this notion of "ecclesiola." The black nuclear family has typically been understood within the broader context of the extended community.

Theologian Melva Costen points to the importance of kinship in the development of African American religious and family life:

> One of the strongest forces in traditional African life that continues among African Americans is a deep sense of kinship and related-

ness. From the perspective of primal world views, God is the continuing source and sustenance of all that is good. Since God called forth the cosmos as an orderly, complete, and perfect entity, all creation and the inhabited universe are sacred to God. Humanity is part of the created order, thus human beings exist in unity with one another and with all of creation. To be human means that one belongs to a family or community ... This understanding of community created by the kinship system is a reminder that individuals exist as a part of the corporate whole.[12]

A distinctive of the black extended family is its multigenerational composition. Although many black extended networks are comprised of a family taking in additional adult siblings or a household absorbing extra nieces and nephews, a significant number of extended families are three-generational households.[13]

C. Eric Lincoln in *The Black Church Since Frazier*, suggests that the black church is the embodiment of the extended family. To understand the power of the black church it must first be understood that there is no disjunction between the black church and the black community. The church is the spiritual face of the black community, and whether one is a "church member" or not is beside the point in any assessment of the importance and meaning of the Black Church.[14]

Wallace Charles Smith suggests that the black family's chief strength remains its extended nature. It is important to note that two skills that have allowed the black family to survive throughout the period of slavery and beyond are its adaptability to change and its extended (rather than nuclear) structure.[15]

According to Smith, to establish a black family theology, one must understand and appreciate these key family strengths. The knowledge of these important family attributes is crucial to the task because the black church is an extension of the black family. Some black liberation theologians, while claiming to be doing theology from below, have too often overlooked the family model as a way of describing the genius of the black church experience.[16]

Any efforts aimed at preserving and strengthening black families could draw upon these strengths and the reestablishment of the critical necessity of family and church cooperation. Historically, the church and family engaged in such cooperation. The black church developed out of the deprivation and oppression experienced during more than 240 years of slavery in America, and has persisted as a support system for the oppressed. Sadly for many blacks, the secularization of the twentieth century has exacted a great price as there now exists a de-emphasis on the critical connection between the African American church and family.

EXPERIENCE

In March 1986, Bill Moyers - then a CBS television correspondent - hosted a controversial documentary on the black family. Moyers interviewed a sampling of teenaged mothers, as well as jobless males who had fathered multiple children. Although the documentary closed by soliciting comments and prescriptions of Black experts, the overall impression many viewers received was that the urban Black family was in a pathological crisis. In the years since the program, journalists, educators, religious leaders, opinion-makers, and public officials have focused increasingly on the problems of the Black family.[17]

Clarence Walker asserts that the African American family and its problems have been the focus of national attention for more than four decades. In *Breaking Strongholds in the African American Family,* he points out that social scientists and mental health specialists, both black and white, have proposed a host of theories and reasons for the problems and challenges of the African American family: (1) The general consensus is that they are the victims of racism; (2) the socio-economic theory suggests that there is a relationship between national economics and the plight of poor black families; (3) the matriarchal legacy theory points to the absence of African American fathers, creating a large group of female-headed, single-parent homes; (4) the Afroism theory implies that the African American family's kinship structure and culture are in conflict with the dominant Eurocentric Anglo-Saxon values in our present society.[18]

In *Troubling Biblical Waters*, Cain Hope Felder points out that de facto secularism, materialism, moral confusion, and chaotic public policies have endangered the stability of all types of families. Sadly, however, some social commentators single out black families and households to highlight the so-called pathology of Black life without mention of the political decisions, socioeconomic policies, and biblical distortions that contribute to the Black condition.[19]

Many agree that one of the great challenges facing African American churches today is developing wholistic approaches to strengthening families. Many black families face issues which are endemic to the broader society, but which often disproportionately affect African American families.

Sociologist Andrew Billingsley offers hope for the future of African American families as the church engages in proactive, visionary approaches that promote the family's preservation. Billingsley suggests that the African American family is neither dead or dying, not vanishing. Instead, the family remains a resilient and adaptive institution reflecting the most basic values, hopes, and aspirations of the descendants of African people in America. But to say that black families are alive is not to say that they are all faring well.[20]

REASON

Cornell West, the author of *Race Matters* refers to the conditions - perceived or real - that pervade African American communities as "nihilism in black America." According to West, nihilism is to be understood not as a philosophic doctrine that there are no rational grounds for legitimate standards or authority; it is far more the lived experience characterized by horrifying meaninglessness; hopelessness; and (most important) lovelessness.[21]

The nihilism of black America is manifest in realities such as disproportionate rates of poverty, unemployment and divorce that affect African American families. It is apparent in deteriorating educational and social systems, along with higher rates of addiction to tobacco, alcohol and many drugs, in addition to generally higher rates of violent crime and incarceration in African American communities.

For religious scholars like West and James Cone, who is perhaps the leading proponent of black liberation theology, theology must be understood from the perspective of the liberation from the realities of nihilism among the least advantaged of society. Thus, to strengthen African

American families and communities becomes one of the loci of liberation theology in America.

Black liberation theology recognizes the historical impact of slavery and the subsequent de facto segregation and Jim Crowism upon the contemporary condition of African American people. In light of this, black liberation theology must also recognize the role that the black church - by virtue of its historical significance as an institution - should play in preserving and strengthening black families.

Theologian Carlyle Fielding Steward suggests that as the primary source of spiritual and social transformation in African American communities, the church will help families see the face of reality. The face of reality, with all its ugliness and pain, must be transfigured into a new awareness of the self and God, and their myriad possibilities.[22]

The theological task of the black church involves the reaffirmation and reappropriation of the indelible link between the African American family and church. Through the prayerful and faithful employment of the resources of Scripture, tradition, experience and reason, both will gain a renewed vision of this union which has served as the central source of strength for black communities over the generations.

§ § §

ENDNOTES

1. Albert Outler, *Theology in the Wesleyan Spirit* (Nashville: Discipleship Resources, 1974), Outler develops the "Wesley Quadrilateral" throughout this and other works.

2. Cain Hope Felder, *Troubling Biblical Waters: Race, Class and Family* (New York: Orbis Books, 1989), p. 5.

3. Ibid., p. 150.

4. Ibid., p. 165.

5. Ibid.

6. John Hope Franklin, *From Slavery to Freedom* (New York: Vintage Books, 1947), The matters of slavery and racism are chronicled throughout the book.

7. E. Franklin Frazier, *The Negro Church in America* (New York: Schocken Books, 1963), p. 13.

8. Wallace Charles Smith, *The Church in the Life of the Black Family* (Valley Forge, PA: Judson Press, 1990), p. 22.

9. Carter G Woodson, *The History of the Negro Church* (Washington, DC: Associated Publishers, 1921), chapter 2.

10. Peter Paris, *The Social Teaching of the Black Churches* (Philadelphia, PA: Fortress Press, 1988), p. 17.

11. J. Deotis Roberts, *Roots of a Black Future: Family and Church* (Philadelphia: The Westminster Press, 1980), p. 24.

12. Melva Costen, *African American Christian Worship* (Nashville: Abingdon Press, 1993), p. 21.

13. Darlene B. Hannah, "The Black Extended Family: An Appraisal of Its Past, Present and Future," in Lee June, ed., *The Black Family: Past, Present and Future*, (Grand Rapids, MI: Zondervan Publishing, 1991), p. 37.

14. C. Eric Lincoln, *The Black Church Since Frazier* (New York: Schocken Books, 1974), p. 115.

15. Smith, p. 22.

16. Ibid.

17. Hank Allen, "The Black Family: Its Unique Legacy, Current Challenges, and Future Prospects," June, ed., p. 17.

18. Clarence Walker, *Breaking Strongholds in the African American Family* (Grand Rapids, MI: Zondervan Press, 1996), p. 9.

19. Felder, p. 150.

20. Andrew Billingsley, *Climbing Jacob's Ladder: The Enduring Legacy of African American Families* (New York: Simon and Schuster, 1992), p. 17.

21. Cornell West, *Race Matters* (Boston: Beacon Press, 1991), p. 14.

22. Carlyle Fielding Stewart, *Joy Songs, Trumpet Blasts, and Hallelujah Shouts: Sermons in the African-American Preaching Tradition* (Lima OH: CSS Publishing, 1997), p. 23.

CONTEMPORARY ISSUES FACING THE AFRICAN AMERICAN CHURCH AND FAMILY

The church continues to struggle to identify approaches and develop strategies to effectively improve African American families, and empower God's people to become all that God would have us to be. It has been the historic role of the black church to provide leadership and resources leading to hopeful solutions over and against the plethora of societal ills faced by African Americans.

Despite earlier efforts of churches to effect positive change in black communities, African American family life today can be characterized as troubled and fractured at the very best - and in many cases dysfunctional. Dr. Cornell West of Harvard University refers to the condition endemic in Black America as "nihilism" - a certain hopelessness which is characterized by a lack of meaning and most importantly a loss of love.[1]
This nihilism is vividly seen in the abject poverty, destructive violence, and inadequate educational and health-care systems that affect many African American families and communities. Nihilism is evident in the disproportionate numbers of African American men locked in prison cells, the disparate numbers of households headed by single mothers, the heroin and crack cocaine that poison the streets, and the children who plan their funerals when - by all rights - they should be preparing for college.

The church faces the task of developing wholistic ministries to address this nihilism - given that many persons have historically looked to the church as a primary source of strength, hope and resource.

Here, the focus is on three issues which, in many ways, epitomize the various social and spiritual concerns facing African American churches and families. The pervasive nature of social ills such as Acquired Immune Deficiency Disease (AIDS), Poverty, and Substance Abuse continue to destroy and weaken family life among African Americans. Certainly, there are various other matters that warrant the church's attention, but in many ways these are representative of the dilemmas facing African American families.

CHAPTER TWO

AIDS: THE DEADLY ENEMY

Of all the health dilemmas facing our society, Acquired Immune Deficiency Syndrome, commonly known as AIDS, is perhaps the most troubling. Because of the expanding number of persons who have died from AIDS, been diagnosed as having the Human Immunodeficiency Virus (HIV-positive), or are currently suffering from various illnesses associated with AIDS, it has become one of our society's greatest and most feared killers.

There remains no known cure for the disease, and it continues to spread in epidemic proportions. Recent data indicates that more than 30 million persons are infected with HIV or AIDS throughout the world, with more than six million being children. In North America, more than 1.5 million persons are infected with HIV/AIDS. The rate of infection is increasing the fastest within the African American community, especially among women and children.[2]

Only a few years ago, a trip to almost any health care facility specializing in AIDS and HIV infection in the United States would have revealed a majority of men who were gay. Making such a trip now, would reveal something quite different: women, children, men and families of many types are affected by HIV/AIDS.[3]

There continue to be many stigmas that add to the various complexities of how to perceive and deal with AIDS. The truth continues to unfold, and perhaps the most glaring fact surrounding the disease is its pervasiveness among persons of all races, genders, ages and socio-economic strata.

One only has to read about or visit a neo-natal ward at virtually any urban hospital to understand the way the suffering of AIDS has permeated our society. The stories of thousands of border babies are well documented. Innocent babies, certainly through no fault of their own, are born HIV-infected, and spend most or all of lives, that are often much too short, confined to hospitals and fighting for their very existence.[4]

As Suzanne Levert suggests in *AIDS: In Search of a Killer*, the human cost of AIDS, in lives, in grief, in pain, in death, and in communities torn apart is beyond calculation.[5]

AIDS involves an ever-widening circle of persons, with ever-increasing costs - socially, politically, economically and spiritually. Given its pervasiveness, I believe it is safe to suggest that all of us have been or will be affected in some way by this disease.

There are many psycho-social, theological and spiritual matters that should be given consideration as the black church deals with increasing occurrences of HIV/AIDS. As a pastor, counselor, nephew and friend of persons who have suffered with the disease, I continue to reflect upon how African American congregations might more wholistically minister with persons and families affected by the disease.

BIBLICAL PERSPECTIVES ON SIN AND DISEASE

The idea that physical disease is caused by a person's sin is an ancient one. In Leviticus 13:14 where the laws on leprosy are set forth, it was the task of the priest, the religious leader, to judge whether or not a person was diseased or healed. This took on the dimensions of determining whether the person was "unclean" or "clean", and whether one was worthy to be a part of the surrounding community.

AIDS is viewed by some as a modern leprosy. By some, it is looked upon as punishment for a sinful, immoral lifestyle. The views of Dr. D. James Kennedy, pastor of the Coral Ridge Presbyterian Church in Ft. Lauderdale, Florida are not atypical of the views of many Christians concerning AIDS and other diseases. In a sermon entitled, "The Bible and AIDS," Kennedy stated:

> "Down through all of the history of this world, God, in his longsuffering and patient kindness, has waited and urged men to repent and return unto him. But, finally the cup of his wrath has been filled to overflowing and he has on numerous occasions poured out his wrath on the country."[6]

Kennedy further cites several biblical examples of plague as punishment. The punishment that God sent for angels sleeping with the sons of men in Genesis 6:5, the destruction of Sodom and Gomorrah, and the plagues that God sent to Israel because of their transgressions while still in the Sinai desert.[7]

Kennedy closes the sermon with an appeal for America to fast and pray for God to remove the "plague" of AIDS. In this he is following standard Biblical precedent. Old Testament prophets urged the people to repent of their sins and even Jesus told his listeners on various occasions to "go and sin no more."[8]

In John 9:1-2 the disciples ask Jesus, "... who sinned, this man or his parents, that he was born blind?" Jesus tempered his counsel with mercy and forgiveness, something that many persons seem reluctant to do relative to AIDS and some of the other forms of suffering in our midst.

It is clear that the notion of an inextricable and direct connection between disease and sin was refuted on many occasions in the words and actions of Jesus. During his ministry, he went about offering healing and wholeness to those who suffered most throughout his world. The theme that runs throughout the life and ministry of Jesus is that God is faithful and persists in loving us, and does not abandon us in the most frightening and desperate situations of life. As the apostle Paul wrote, "nothing can separate us from the love of God in Christ Jesus" (Romans 8:39).

PSYCHOSOCIAL DIMENSIONS OF AIDS

One only has to talk with someone experiencing symptoms related to HIV and AIDS to recognize the tremendous psychological and social impact of the disease. Most people are not prepared to deal with the reality of sickness and death in early adulthood. It is painful to see young people robbed of the energy we expect of youth. It is difficult to talk with a young man or woman who faces the prospect of not seeing his or her children grow up. It is sad to talk about funeral arrangements instead of new careers, families, and long-range plans. And it is difficult to hear and attempt to respond to the perplexing questions of "why, why me, and why now?"

Certainly, there is a plethora of complicated and demanding psychological issues raised by the spectrum of HIV and AIDS. The threat of fatal illness and physical pain, as well as issues surrounding death itself place immense stress upon the psyche. Elisabeth Kubler-Ross, a psychiatrist renown for her work in the areas of death and dying, was one of the first persons within the medical community to look closely at the psycho-social and spiritual dimensions of AIDS. She considered her early work with AIDS victims to be a natural outgrowth of her work in death and dying. In her book *AIDS: The Ultimate Challenge*, Kubler-Ross prophetically wrote in 1987:

> "... we can no longer deny that AIDS is a life threatening illness that will eventually involve millions of people and decimate large proportions of our human population; it is our choice to grow and learn from it, to either help the people with this disease or abandon them. It is our choice to live up to this ultimate challenge or perish."[9]

AIDS is essentially a matter of death and dying, and it calls upon all of a person's (and their loved ones') psychological resources to cope and come to grips with the meaning and reality of the experience.

Perhaps, the most obvious and pervasive psychosocial issue surrounding HIV/AIDS is fear. AIDS is more feared than cancer, heart disease, or even auto accidents, which all continue to kill more people per year than AIDS. Mounting concern about the disease is visible daily. People who have tested positive have been fired from jobs, evicted from apartments, refused seats on airplanes, and denied access to public facilities.

Persons who are HIV-positive or who are experiencing the effects of full-blown AIDS may face a variety of different fears. These include: (1) Fear of what being HIV-positive means; (2) Fear of the hospital and health-care delivery system; (3) Fear of what others will think; and (4) Fear of being alone to face the crisis.

Psychologist Susan Fair points out that there are various emotional issues that should be considered. Emotional reactions to a diagnosis of HIV seropositivity, HIV-related disease, or AIDS come in as many varieties as there are people. Each person generally reacts in a way that is consistent with his or her personality and typical style of coping with stress. However, two issues seem to present themselves at one time or another to almost all who are infected, regardless of their personal coping style. These issues, simply stated, are feelings of powerlessness and isolation. The nature of the disease, its fatality, the stigmatization of those infected, and the fear of contagion, all make powerlessness and isolation very real concerns for most people who are infected and also for those who care about and treat them.[10]

Perhaps the most obvious sociological issues involve the stigmatization of those who have been diagnosed. Many questions surface as a result: "Why the stigma?". "What causes people to recoil in horror, at the mere mentioning of the word "AIDS?" "What causes us, who are more educated and knowledgeable than any group of people in the history of civilization, to react much like the people in biblical times as they shunned the lepers?"

There are several reasons for the stigmatization surrounding the disease. First, there remains a great deal of confusion over what is actually known. Although scientists and medical professionals continue to stress that the AIDS virus cannot be transmitted through casual contact, the attitude of many people seems to be, "I'd rather be safe than sorry ... I don't want to be the first person to die because of casual contact with a person who has the disease."

Secondly, although it is spreading among heterosexuals, the disease still disproportionately affects those who are considered to be outside the mainstream of our society, such as homosexuals, Blacks, Hispanics, drug abusers and the poor. The prevailing thought seems to be that AIDS is not a disease that will affect the lives of "normal" people, and thus there are many in "mainstream" America who choose not to associate themselves with the disease on any level.

Thirdly, the disease forces us to think about the routes of transmittal and the intricacies of important bodily functions. Sexual intercourse and blood transfusions, two primary means of transmission for the HIV virus, are typically viewed as life-giving transactions between human beings. Intravenous drugs are used in medical settings to save lives. With AIDS, these same acts result in suffering and death. It seems easier for many in our society to deny the pervasiveness of AIDS than to confront its very real presence in the lives of virtually all people.

Fourth, the stigmatization surrounding AIDS continues because the disease must be dealt with as a terminal disease that continues to have no known cure. In his book, *Mortal Fear: Meditations on Death and AIDS*, John Snow points out that AIDS must be viewed not merely as another disease, but as a terminal disease. Concerning the nature of terminal disease, Snow writes:

> "If our disease turns out to be terminal, the sense of excommunication becomes intense. In our empirical, problem-solving society where it is assumed that if we set the problem correctly we can solve it, we find ourselves in a situation which may have no problem-solving significance ... Dying in our society seems to be something strange, surprising, alien to all we have learned about living."[11]

THE SPIRITUAL DIMENSIONS OF AIDS

In our attempts to address the tremendous psycho-social effects of AIDS, we must also consider the spiritual dimensions of the disease. Perhaps, one of the most important considerations for the continuing spiritual journey of persons experiencing grief associated with HIV/AIDS is the knowledge that there is a community that is present to care for them.

The church is called to be such a community, sharing the message of grace, mercy and unconditional love that God has offered through His only begotten son, Jesus Christ (John 3:16).

Historically, the African American church has served as a form of vital community. Thus, African American churches in contemporary society should be informed of the perplexities and pervasiveness of the AIDS epidemic, and how it affects individuals, families and communities. Churches must come to understand their role in reaching out to those who are suffering.

Jesus taught us that all persons are intrinsically valuable in God's eyes, and because God loves all of us unconditionally and completely, all of humanity can experience God's care, compassion and wholeness even in the midst of adversity, pain and death.

In light of this, the church is called to model the wholistic ministry that Jesus demonstrated. The model of ministry as taught by Jesus is one that was directed particularly toward the marginalized: those persons with needs that various other societal institutions failed to address. This was especially evident in the various instances where Jesus healed those who were suffering from physical maladies. He taught us that the commonality of our human strengths and frailties far transcend our many human diversities.

At Ames United Methodist Church, I was preceded as the pastor by a young man who became infected and eventually died from AIDS. I remember the tragic and grief-filled situation I encountered when arriving and meeting congregants. A "hush-hush" atmosphere permeated the congregation; a collective disappointment and distrust seemed pervasive.

In the days and weeks leading up to Karl's death, members of the congregation would say nothing of the nature of his illness and impending death. There was some murmuring that he might have "cancer", but it became the church's silent secret that the specific illness that Karl was experiencing was AIDS.

In the black church, there seems to be a collective inability and/or unwillingness to discuss HIV/AIDS in all of its dimensions. There seems to be no clear theology or praxis of how to minster with those affected by the disease. To my recollection, the word "AIDS" was never mentioned at Karl's funeral.

This experience with AIDS did eventually result in Ames Church being able to grieve Karl's death by sharing stories of his life and ministry, and ultimately beginning to move forward in the development of a theology of AIDS, in particular - and terminal illness, in general. God's grace, the affirmation of our human creation in God's image and goodness, and the focus on community have always been - and continue to be - critical constructs within the African American church.

The church must be willing to take the often unknown and risky journey into the lives of those who suffer. As faith communities, churches are called to convey through deed and word, the message that God is the source of strength and hope. By affirming the presence of God and community amidst suffering, death and grief -comfort, hope and holistic healing become possible.

THE BLACK FAMILY   19

Churches can help persons dealing with AIDS grow spiritually through a number of means. These might include opportunities and resources for meditating, reading sacred texts and other literature, and offering group activities that nurture the spirit and provide support. One very effective example of an activity to support persons suffering with AIDS is the "Quality of Life" retreats sponsored by United Methodist clergy and laity in the Baltimore, MD-Washington, DC region. These retreats serve as periodic gatherings of hope, love and support for HIV-infected persons. In such gatherings persons experience the importance of the community of faith and the reality of the family of God in the midst of the grief process. (See Appendix 1)

§ § §

ENDNOTES

1. West, p. 14.

2. Data compiled by the United Nations and released on Thursday, November 27, 1997. This information is excerpted from an article in the *Washington Post*, dated November 28, 1997.

3. Rob Vaughn, "The Changing Face of AIDS," *The Virginia United Methodist Advocate* (Richmond: Virginia United Methodist Publications, 1990), p. 3.

4. Vaughn, p. 5.

5. Suzanne Levert, *AIDS: In Search of a Killer* (New York: Julian Messner, 1987), p. 115.

6. "The Bible and AIDS," a sermon by Dr. James Kennedy, Coral Ridge Presbyterian Church, Fort Lauderdale, FL, as quoted in the *Military Chaplains' Review, Spring 1988* (Washington, DC: US Army Chaplaincy Services Support Agency, Military Chaplains' Review, 1988), p. 3.

7. Ibid.

8. Ibid.

9. Elisabeth Kubler-Ross *AIDS: The Ultimate Challenge* (New York: MacMillan Publishing Company, 1987), p. 20.

10. Susan M. Fair, "Neuropsychosocial Complications of HIV; Information and Interventions for Caregivers", *Military Chaplains' Review, Spring 1988* (Washington, DC: US Army Chaplaincy Services Support Agency, 1988), p. 58.

11. John Snow, *Mortal Fear: Meditations on Death and AIDS* (Cambridge, MA: Cowley Publications, 1987), p. 7.

CHAPTER THREE

POVERTY: The Effects of Economic Injustice On African Americans

Economic injustice in America can be seen, perhaps most vividly, by looking at the injustice of poverty. More than 33 million Americans - about one in every seven people in our nation - are poor by the government's official estimates. Some people are poor because they work hard but do not make enough to support their families. Others are poor because they cannot find jobs.[1]

The injustice of poverty is heightened by the gap between the working poor and the idle rich. The gap between the rich and the poor in the United States is enormous: more than half the total net wealth is held by the richest 10 percent of families, while the bottom 20 percent of families receives less than 5 percent of the nation's total income.[2]

The rates of poverty in America are highest among those who have borne the brunt of racial prejudice and discrimination. Black Americans are about three times more likely to be poor than white Americans. While one of every nine white Americans is poor, one out of every three black Americans is poor.[3]

Long-term poverty is concentrated among racial minorities and families headed by women. African-American children are the largest group among the poor.[4] Most families with poor children receive no government assistance, have no health insurance, and cannot pay their medical bills.[5]

One of the most profound realities about the problem of poverty is that the vast majority of those who are poor in America are working persons with children. Because of a complex array of circumstances, these persons find themselves fighting through the cycles of poverty that affect every aspect of life.

Much of today's national political debate seems to be driven by one fundamental question, "What should society be doing for the poor?" We hear of poverty - and essentially our inability to comprehend and address it - in the thinly veiled debates on welfare reform. We witness society's collective grappling with poverty in the calls for the elimination of affirmative action, as well in the moves to make significant cuts in funding for medicare and public education, and even in the debate over whether or not there is a need to build more prisons.

Indeed, it seems that the increasingly popular societal view is that the majority of the poor are lazy, shiftless, and even unconcerned about their own well-being. We hear this in the discussion about "welfare mothers who (supposedly) don't want to work ... and just want to live off the government." We hear it in the discussions about "those lazy, homeless men, who (supposedly) would rather beg on street corners than get a job, and find a decent place to live."

Those who have never been poor may not be able to understand the experiences of the child who has no food to eat or clothing to wear, and thus chooses to stay home from school rather than face the ridicule of peers. Those who have not experienced poverty may not understand the mother who makes the choice to stay home rather than work for the minimum wage in a dead-end job, especially in the light of escalating day-care expenses and the rise of other costs related to employment.

Poverty is everywhere with us. And for those who are blessed with some modicum of well-being, it can become temptingly easy to become removed from the problem. It is enticing to fail to see ourselves in the faces and bodies of those who have the least among us. It can become convenient to dismiss the problem of poverty and to deny any responsibility that we might have as individuals and churches for its alleviation.

THE SPIRITUAL DIMENSIONS OF POVERTY

It is clear in reading the Gospels that Jesus had a profound and abiding concern for the poor. We recall that Jesus declared that "what you do to the least among these my sisters and brothers, you do the same to me" (Matthew 25:45).

According to Dr. Martin Luther King, Jr. poverty results not from a lack of resources, but from the unequal distribution of existing resources. Many of the social ills that affect African Americans are directly rooted in poverty and economic deprivation. The church and gospel that focuses solely on spiritual needs without regard for social and economic realities is ignoring the necessity for wholistic ministry in African American communities.

Thus, the church should be significantly concerned about how those who are poor are portrayed and treated throughout our society. Unfortunately, when particular constituencies within the church have demonstrated material and spiritual needs, the reactions of prevailing power structures have often resulted in a "reaching and looking down" rather than a "reaching and looking across." This "reaching and looking down" provides for short-term provisions to those in need, but generally fails to facilitate empowerment of needy constituencies to provide for themselves in the long-run.

At the Fifth Assembly of the World Council of Churches, the matter of long-term empowerment of the poor was addressed. The development process should be understood as a liberating process aimed at justice, self-reliance and economic growth.[6]

Gilbert Caldwell, in his book, *Race, Racism and Reconciliation*, poignantly offers that the church must discover ways to "be in solidarity with the poor" among us. The church must remember to act on what it believes. Caldwell goes on to state:

> We believe God is creator and parent. God is an equal opportunity creator and parent. We are not created by God to be rich or poor, powerful or powerless. We of the church believe that every creature on this earth was created by God and we thus share the same parent, and we are brothers and sisters. We must see to it that our brothers and sisters do not suffer. When they suffer, we must suffer.[7]

It is the church's divine calling to convey, through its thoughts, words and actions, that God is indeed "for the poor" - those who Jesus referred to as "the least of these."

As churches move into solidarity with the poor, this might lead us to re-evaluate our views of those who - for whatever reasons - find themselves in various forms of economic distress whether it be hunger, homelessness, unemployment, under-education, or the lack of adequate health-care.

What does God require of the church? Programs which provide shelter for the homeless, food for the hungry, clothes for the naked, holistic health services, legal aid, remedial and continuing education, job skills training, counseling, day-care for working parents, and substance abuse services are often considered to be outside the scope of the church's evangelistic mission. But as Jesus reminded Peter, our love of Christ is best demonstrated in the world through service with, and empowerment of those who are oppressed (John 21:15-17).

Clearly, God requires that the church not only believes in equality, but that it acts out equality and justice by developing approaches and promoting those means that will lead to poverty's eradication. As in the days of Christ, it will have to be the people of faith who will stand for those who are disenfranchised and marginalized among us.

And so, what should be the black church's approach to dealing with poverty, given its pervasive presence in African American communities? Gilbert Caldwell points out some of the specific ways that Christians can be in solidarity with the poor. First, we must acknowledge that too often we represent the problem rather than the solution. Second, we must be honest about who we are, what we do, what is important to us, in terms of our lifestyle. Third, we must be consistent and persevering. Our faith does not give us the right to burn out. Fourth, we must be willing to critique systems. Fifth, we must be positive and hopeful because the gospel of the church is a gospel of hope.[8]

These thoughts can translate directly into churches developing wholistic ministries to help in eradicating poverty. It is clear that churches remain a major means of empowerment in black communities. Many churches are now discovering that is advantageous to pool their resources into collective banking, cooperative housing and other resourcing opportunities which serve as an impetus for economic development in African American communities.

At Ames Church, we engaged in a number of ministries aimed at dealing with poverty and promoting economic development. One was participation in a regional food bank which allowed the church to pool its donations with other churches, thus facilitating the service of far more persons than any one church could serve. Secondly, the church sought to address the issue of the lack of affordable housing in the community by offering educational programs which helped lead people toward becoming eligible to purchase their own homes through non-profit housing agencies. Thirdly, the church sponsored regular job fairs and maintained a data base on available employment opportunities throughout the community. Several persons were employed through their involvement in the church, and this sharing of job information.

§ § §

ENDNOTES

1. Karen Lebacqz, *Justice in an Unjust World* (Minneapolis: Augsburg Publishing House, 1987), p. 28.

2. Ibid.

3. National Conference of Catholic Bishops, *Economic Justice for All* (Washington, DC: National Conference of Catholic Bishops, 1986), p. 8.

4. American Humane Association, Children's Division, "Fact Sheet" (Englewood, Colorado, 1998; Information provided by the Children's Defense Fund, 1997).

5. National Conference of Catholic Bishops, p. 8.

6. Gilbert H. Caldwell, *Race, Racism and Reconciliation* (Philadelphia: Simon Printing and Publishing, Inc., 1989), p. 32.

7. Ibid., p. 33.

8. Ibid., p. 34.

CHAPTER FOUR

ADDICTION: Substance Abuse and African American Families

African American churches should give careful attention to the effects of drug and alcohol addiction on African American families. Inspite of the growing number of therapeutic and social service resources available to deal with addiction and the related behaviors, churches typically have been unable or have refused to wholistically address the problem.

One of the primary reasons for this inability or refusal seems to be denial. United Methodist Bishop Felton Edwin May of Washington, DC summed up the problem of denial. "We seem to deny that there is a problem in our churches. Denial is defined as a defensive process whereby painful thoughts and feelings associated with reality are unconsciously rejected or evaded."[1]

The fact is that there are persons attending our churches who are looking for ways to deal with and overcome their addictions. A major factor in denial is that persons in church are not always comfortable with admitting there is a problem with their members. Another problem is that churches seem to experience some difficulty in articulating a theology of grace in light of the terrible effects of addictive behaviors.

It is important for churches to take an in-depth look at the various theological and pragmatic aspects of substance abuse and addiction. Given the increasing rates of addiction in black communities - and the incumbent problems, including violence and health concerns - the question is, "How can churches employ theological, spiritual, social, psychological and the other resources at its disposal in helping to eradicate addiction in African American communities?"

It was during a field placement at the Johns Hopkins-Bayview Hospital Drug and Alcohol Treatment Facility in Baltimore, MD in 1995 that I was exposed to an environment in which I could concretely grapple with the issues of how black churches might wholistically address the problem of substance abuse. While working with clients who were being treated for addiction to drugs and alcohol, I explored some of the possibilities of how integrative approaches to health-care related to the ministries of the black church.

While at Johns Hopkins, one of the first, and perhaps most important discoveries was that in my professional ministerial responsibilities as the pastor of Ames United Methodist Church, as well as in my role as a teacher and consultant with various institutions, I had often been insulated and isolated from the magnitude of the realities of suffering that occurs among people dealing with addiction.

Within the church, the common modality for addressing the vicissitudes of the suffering related to addiction is commonly one which can be described as a "band-aid approach." The church's common practice is to direct its energies toward addressing the immediate concern, but seldom are there comprehensive strategies for addressing the overall, long-term health and wholeness of persons.

This may be attributed - at least to some degree - to a collective lack of vision in terms of the church's ability to articulate the concept of wholistic ministry, given the need to address the spiritual, along with the physical and intellectual needs of persons.

THE SPIRITUAL DIMENSIONS OF SUBSTANCE ABUSE

The ministry of Jesus focused upon addressing the actual physical, as well as spiritual needs of the persons he encountered. Jesus went from town to town ministering with those in his midst who were suffering with various forms of infirmity, and offering hope and healing to those experiencing the effects of sickness and pain.

The health of persons must be understood as a critical component of the faith journey upon which the church invites persons to engage. Kenneth Bakken, in his book *The Call to Wholeness: Health as a Spiritual Journey* affirms the notion that health indeed plays a critical role in leading persons toward wholeness in their spiritual lives. Bakken offers a critique of the present health-care environment relative to the church and society:

> We are faced with a crisis the proportions of which are just beginning to be realized by the medical, theological, and socio-

political structures and institutions world wide. There is a crisis of confidence not only in the persons in leadership positions but also in the failing solutions to increasingly urgent needs. The daily litany of crime, disease, starvation, war, threat of nuclear destruction, inflation, and pollution, to name a few, is lethal to the human person. This lack of confidence certainly can deaden any creative responses, as we simply and unthinkingly mouth stock answers based upon a world view that is no longer valid.[2]

Through the experience at the Johns Hopkins Drug Treatment Facility, I discovered that many of the clients who were dealing with the problems of substance abuse (drug and/or alcohol addiction) had some profound notion of faith in their lives. It was somewhat surprising to find that institutional religion had played at least a cursory role in the lives of many of those who were engaged in treatment. In the context of my counseling and interviews with clients, I discovered that many had been very involved in the life of the church at some point, and believed that they had somehow "lost their way." Many expressed that they were now searching to experience and know God in new ways.

Many African American clients seemed to be profoundly frustrated and disappointed that the teachings and knowledge that they had attained in black churches had not necessarily resulted in a closer walk with God for them. While some acknowledged and affirmed various tenets of the Christian faith, many, for any number of reasons, expressed the sentiment that the church and its teachings had become irrelevant, and that religion was otherwise unable to address the perplexity of their current plight in any coherent and substantive manner.

However, there also appeared to be a certain earnestness etched in the persevering spirit and hope among many of those suffering in the midst of substance abuse. There seemed to be the persistent hope that the Scriptures and doctrine to which they had been exposed in black churches, would some day result in substantive change and growth in their lives. This earnestness and hope was evident in the number of persons who continued to attend worship services while involved in the very intensive recovery program at Johns Hopkins.

Many clients would leave the hospital at lunch-time or in the evenings to attend church services. In the midst of their struggling and searching, many continued to discover hope in the black church. Some spoke of the message of hope, and the promise of joy heard in the sermons and songs of the churches they attended, and expressed the desire that such words would help them on the path to recovery.

In discussions and interviews with clients regarding the role that churches could play in their ongoing recovery, many indicated that frustrations begin, and a void occurs, when the church's actions do not provide the ministry to follow their words. In other words, the church often does not "practice what it preaches" and does not "walk its talk." Thus, persons may come to view the message of the possibility of resurrection and new life that is promised through Christ as somewhat shallow and hypothetical, if not hypocritical.

There seems to be a general inability of churches to adequately articulate and appropriate a theology of suffering in relation to addiction. Seldom are clear and concise connections made between spirituality and suffering in ways that affect real change in the lives of God's people. Gustavo Gutierrez speaks of this dilemma in *On Job: God-talk and the Suffering of the Innocent*:

> This then is the question: Are suffering human beings able to enter into an authentic relationship with God and find a correct way of speaking about God? If the answer is yes, then it will be a priori possible to do the same in other human situations. But if the answer is no, then it will be irrelevant that persons living in less profound and challenging situations "appear" to accept the gratuitousness of God's love and claim to practice a disinterested religion. Human suffering is the harsh, demanding ground on which the wager about talk of God is made; it is also that which ensures that the wager has universal applicability.[3]

One of the processes used at the Johns Hopkins Drug and Alcohol Treatment Facility aimed at assisting clients in coming to grips with the matter of suffering was the technique of logotherapy as enumerated by Viktor Frankl in *Man's Search for Meaning*. According to Frankl's logotherapy, we can discover meaning in life in three different ways: (1) by creating a work or doing a deed; (2) by experiencing something or encountering someone; and (3) by the attitude we take toward unavoidable suffering.[4]

Concerning the matter of unavoidable suffering Frankl offers that:

> We must never forget that we may also find meaning in life even when confronted with a hopeless situation, when facing a fate that cannot be changed. For what then matters is to bear witness to the uniquely human potential at its best, which is to transform a personal tragedy into triumph, to turn one's predicament into a human achievement. When we are no longer able to change a situation - just think of an incurable disease such as inoperable cancer - we are challenged to change ourselves ... In some way, suffering ceases to be suffering at the moment that it finds meaning, such as the meaning of a sacrifice.[5]

In the care and ministry of those who are drug addicted - aside from involvement in various derivations of Alcoholics Anonymous and Narcotics Anonymous - churches have generally been unable to develop adequate wholistic strategies for addressing this critical and pervasive health concern, and the suffering experienced by families that is one of the major by-products of drug and alcohol addiction.

A CHURCH-BASED MODEL: "CHRISTIANS IN RECOVERY"

As a result of the insights gleaned at Johns Hopkins Hospital, we at Ames United Methodist Church developed a church-based substance abuse program to address the drug problem in our church and community. "Christians in Recovery" was a Christ-centered, Scripture-based support and recovery program that sought to assist people in the church and community. (see appendix 2)

While the foundation of Christians in Recovery was a Christ-centered, Scripture based twelve-step recovery model, the program focused on each of the five steps of the healing process: (1) prevention, (2) education, (3) intervention, (4) treatment, and (5) recovery. The church worked with county government agencies and private institutions to provide services which included counseling and referral services provided by the pastor and other professionally trained staff, prevention, education and employment assistance.

The "Christians in Recovery" program was ecumenical in its scope, and churches from throughout the community were invited to hold meetings at their churches or to send persons to the meetings held at Ames Church. The success of the program can be measured in that several persons continue to experience recovery, and some have become active members of Ames Church and other churches in the community.

§ § §

ENDNOTES

1. Felton Edwin May, "Yes, You Do Have a Drug Problem in Your Church," *The Circuit Rider* (Nashville: The United Methodist Ppublishing House, March 1994), p. 12.

2. Kenneth L. Bakken, *The Call to Wholeness, Health as a Spiritual Journey* (New York: Crossroad Publishing Company, 1992), p. 33.

3. Gustavo Gutierrez, *On Job: God-talk and the Suffering of the Innocent* (Maryknoll, NY: Orbis Books, 1985), p. 15.

4. Victor Frankl, *Man's Search for Meaning* (New York: Washington Square Press, 1984), p. 135.

5. Ibid.

PART TWO

PRINCIPLES FOR THE CHURCH'S ROLE IN AFRICAN AMERICAN FAMILY PRESERVATION

PART TWO

PRINCIPLES FOR THE CHURCH'S ROLE IN AFRICAN AMERICAN FAMILY PRESERVATION

As the church engages in ministry, it must have clear biblical, theological, social, as well as cultural understandings of its identity as the people of God. Perhaps, the way to attain and maintain this clarity of identity and purpose is by constantly reflecting upon the grace, acts, character, and purpose of God's act in the Person of the Lord Jesus Christ.

The church's mission is to serve the whole people of God. Jesus instructed his disciples to "Go therefore and make disciples of all nations, baptizing them in the name of the Father, the Son, and the Holy Spirit" (Matthew 28:19). In the Great Commission, we discover the church's evangelistic purpose in sharing Christ with others.

Ministry is first and foremost service in and for the church and its members. Before the church can look out into the society for answers, or reach out to evangelize the unchurched, it must first prayerfully, introspectively and critically evaluate how faithfully and effectively it engages in ministry within.

Any strategy for ministry should be specific in its scope, but more importantly must be undergirded by certain biblical-theological principles. Thus, the objective in this section will be to develop biblically and theologically based principles that specifically address the needs of families in black churches.

In the model for the church's role in African American family preservation, an important assumption is that the principles and considerations for Christian ministry cross denominational lines. Therefore, the principles are not constrained, or strictly applied to a particular faith community. In this sense, principles for ministry are universal and can be applied within the context of various African American Christian faith communities. Indeed the community that is authentically Christian has only "One Lord, one faith, and one baptism" (Ephesians 4:5).

In developing principles for wholistic ministry with black families, it might be helpful to reflect on various perspectives on the essential characteristics or "marks" of the Christian church. This helps us to see those constructs and processes that should exist within a faith community for it to be considered authentically church. The question that arises is, "What elements are essential and indispensable for the church as it engages in ministry?"

The Nicene Creed (325 A.D.) contains the familiar words, "I believe in ... one, holy, catholic (universal), and apostolic church." That the church is one, holy, universal, and apostolic have come to be known as the "classic" marks of the Christian church.

Dorothee Solle, the author of *Thinking About God*, offers a more contemporary theory as to the church's characteristics. Solle asserts that the church must be a body of proclamation (kerygma), service/mission (diaconia), and fellowship (koinonia).[1]

If any of these three characteristics are absent from the faith community, then Solle maintains that the body's identity as a Christian church must be brought into question.

I believe that an analysis and appropriation of these seven characteristics can help churches develop a foundation for an effective model of ministry with African American families. Therefore, the development of principles around these characteristics (the church's unity, holiness, universality, apostolicity, kerygma (proclamation/worship), diaconia (service), and koinonia (fellowship)) will be used as a guide in constructing a model for the church's role in African American family preservation.

§ § §

ENDNOTES

1. Dorothee Solle, *Thinking About God: An introduction to Theology* (Philadelphia: Trinity Press International, 1990), p. 141.

CHAPTER FIVE

PRINCIPLE ONE: **Unity**

Ministry Should Be Inclusive In Its Context,
As The Oneness Of The Church Is Affirmed

The model of ministry as taught to the world by Jesus Christ is one of inclusive service in the kingdom of God. Jesus came proclaiming that "the kingdom God is at hand" (Luke 11:20; 21:31). The ministry of Jesus was directed particularly toward those marginalized persons whose needs were not addressed in other sectors of society. By feeding the hungry, healing the sick, raising the dead, ministering with the sinners in his midst, and teaching in parables as to the realities of God's compassion, love, grace, and mercy, Christ clearly pointed to the commonality of our human strengths and weaknesses.

In this commonality we discover unity in Christ. The biblical record makes it clear that Christ intended for the church to be a unified body. Some of the Lord's final words in his prayer for all believers were "That they may be one" (John 17:21). It is incumbent upon the church to share the good news and hope of our unity in Christ in the church and throughout the world.

In light of God's ideal of individual and communal wholeness, the church is called to be the Body of Christ (I Corinthians 12:27). Each member of the Body is connected to the others, as branches are connected to their root or vine. As Christ's body, we are connected - by faith - to each other in, for, and because of Christ, the true vine (John 15:1).

The Body of Christ is then seen as an organic and living entity, dependent upon its vine as the source of its being - its energy. And as the body is dependent upon the vine for its life, it is also dependent upon each of its members, or branches.

The nature of the members within the church, is that each is intricately related and dependent upon the other members of the Body. In this way, members of the Body of Christ can be viewed as more than appendages, like the arms and legs of the human body. Instead, it has been suggested that it might be more appropriate to view members of the Body of Christ as "membranes", where relationships are intertwined and interdependent with the other "membranes" that comprise the Body. The unity that we share in the Spirit of Christ allows us to see our common opportunities to experience the grace of God in our lives.

The Body of Christ, then is a reconciling and healing body -a change agent - that seeks perpetually to bridge the gap between a broken humanity and a gracious God, for the betterment of the church and world.

As it models unity, the black church helps African American families live in cohesion and harmony. At Ames United Methodist Church, unity in Christ was affirmed and appropriated through the consistent focus on the church as the family of God. Each ministry was viewed as a smaller part of a more important whole. Ministry teams and committees within the church were encouraged to model unity, even amidst the growing diversity of gifts that was in our midst.

Ministries which promote unity can be developed around the church's vision. At Ames Church, our vision statement served to unify us and place the church on one accord as we focused on our purpose in what God was calling us to become. Unity was consistently encouraged in carrying out each of the ministries embodied in the Vision Statement (see Appendix 3).

The Ames Vision Statement is:

> "We, the members of Ames United Methodist Church, are blessed and Spirit-led Christians. Our purpose is to know God through the ministries of worship, study and service. By loving, praying and evangelizing, we seek to touch the lives of our families, communities and all God's people."

In light of the common ground that all Christians share, the gifts, graces, skills and talents of those who are a part of the family of God must be nurtured and developed with the realization that ministry has to focus on individual persons and their needs. Here, the African American church is called to identify particular gifts and needs, seeking to then minister in the context of the communal witness.

The apostle Paul affirmed the diversity of gifts and needs when he told the Corinthian Church, "Now there are varieties of gifts, but the same spirit;

THE BLACK FAMILY 39

and there are varieties of services, but the same Lord; and there are varieties of activities, but the same God who activates all of them in everyone. To each is given the manifestation of the Spirit for the common good" (1 Corinthians 12:4-7).

Certainly, many persons enter local churches today with gifts, interests and concerns which may be considered unique and "non-traditional". Many may not have been in the fellowship of a church for several years, and some may not have been exposed to Christianity and Biblical teachings at all. It is here that the church must be careful to avoid the temptation of ministering solely "to" their needs, and must also seek to minister "with" persons. Persons are not simply recipients of the ministry of Christ, but become active and contributing participants in Christ's ministry, as well.

CHAPTER SIX

PRINCIPLE TWO: **Holiness**

Ministry Should Offer An Understanding
Of The Church As The Holy People Of God

In its ministry, the church should clearly appropriate what it means to be and live holy in light of our creation in God's image (imago dei), and must persistently seek to articulate the intent for humanity to move toward wholeness (shalom) within the context of this holiness. The apostle Paul's words to the Roman church could be insightful for us today, "I appeal to you therefore, bothers and sisters, by the mercies of God, to present your bodies as a living sacrifice, holy and acceptable to God, which is your spiritual worship" (Romans 12:1).

Holiness is God's standard for Christian living. The benefits of holy living can be found in Joshua 3:5. As the people of Israel were preparing to cross the Jordan River, they were instructed, "Sanctify yourselves, for tomorrow the Lord will do wonders among you." As God prepares to move in human lives, the requirement is that persons are sanctified (made holy and set apart) for the work of God.

Within the context of ministry, opportunities should be taken to invite persons into a personal, life-changing relationship with Christ. It was helpful for the Ames Church family to consider what it meant that God was calling us to holy living. In the church's various ministries - including biblical studies, fellowship gatherings and worship experiences - this became an important theme for the church. We were all encouraged to consider our holiness as not merely a "church activity" which was reserved only for Sunday mornings - but we were challenged to consider how we could actualize holiness as an everyday activity and discipline in our lives.

The focus on holy living became particularly important for those who would become new members, and affirm faith in Christ for the first time. It was important for the church to convey that the promise for unchurched and unsaved persons lies in the reality that once they have affirmed faith in Christ, God wills to move persons into lives of holiness and wholeness. As Paul shared with the church at Corinth, "... If anyone be in Christ, there is a new creation: everything old has passed away; see, everything has become new" (II Corinthians 5:17).

In terms of holiness, the issues of evangelization and salvation are of primary concern to the church. At the heart of the church's mission is evangelization. This is the process by which the gospel of Jesus Christ is shared, and persons enter into a personal relationship with Christ and his church.

Evangelization is the entire process by which persons are introduced to the saving power of Christ. This is made clear in Acts 8:34-40, in the account of Philip's encounter with the Ethiopian eunuch. The Christ-sharing act of Philip was one of interpersonal evangelization - of one-to-one sharing and proclaiming Christ in order that the Ethiopian might come to pronounce, "I believe that Jesus Christ is the Son of God" (Acts 8:37b).

In evangelization, the church is called to articulate the meaning of salvation in light of the kingdom of God. In the Scriptures, the kingdom of God is nothing less than the sphere of salvation. Salvation in the Bible means more than turning to God (a conversion). It also carries the connotation of living to God (holiness). The gospel is an invitation to "live to God - submitting our lives to the rule of God in all respects.

Soteriology, the study of the nature of Christian salvation, is based primarily upon the notion that God's gracious act in Jesus Christ was one of reconciling the world that had become alienated and separated from God to God-self (II Corinthians 5:18). God sent Jesus to dwell among humanity in order to save us from sin and separation. Through Christ, we experience God's work of saving grace and move toward lives of holiness.

At Ames Church we sought to develop a wholistic approach to evangelization, salvation and holy living. While leading persons toward a personal relationship with Christ is the primary goal of evangelization, a wholistic understanding of salvation also addresses the physical, social and psychological needs of persons and families. In this way, evangelization serves as a powerful means by which the church can address the plethora of social ills facing African American families.

In order for the reconciliation between humanity and God to occur, we must believe that Jesus Christ is Lord and Savior of the world and of our lives.

This requires a level of personal and long-term commitment on the part of all who consider themselves to be a part of the church. Personal and long-term commitment is particularly challenging for churches in contemporary society. Many African American churches today experience difficulty attracting and retaining persons. Many persons seem to be hesitant about making long-term commitments, including those involving the church.

Some who have studied contemporary culture contend that a possible reason for this is that the liberating and transforming power of a personal relationship with Jesus Christ - a relationship that is fundamentally spiritual amidst the materialism of the contemporary world - may be viewed as too complex, confusing and abstract for many who have been heretofore unchurched.

But given the challenges experienced throughout African American communities today, many persons now seem to be turning to the church for answers as to the meaning of life.

The African American church must remain intentional and persistent in helping persons address the important matter of holiness. When it assumes that persons are not spiritually, emotionally, or socially prepared or willing to make life-long commitments to Christ, the church is failing to fully live out its calling. In addition to programmatic strategies to reach and attract persons, the church should develop balanced, biblical approaches to addressing issues such as evangelization, salvation, and holiness in the context of its ministries.

CHAPTER SEVEN

PRINCIPLE THREE: Catholicity (Universality)
Ministry Should Be Universal In Its Context And Scope

The church has been commissioned by Christ to offer the gospel to all humanity. In the New Testament, it was Jesus' intent that the church would be a universal body. We recall that in the Great Commission, Jesus instructed His disciples to "Go therefore and make disciples of all nations, baptizing them in the name of the Father, and of the Son, and of the Holy Spirit" (Matthew 28:19).

Implicit in the church's universality is the Greek concept 'oikoumene', from which the word ecumenics is derived. In the Great Commandment, Jesus instructed the Pharisees that, "You shall love the Lord your God with all your heart, and with all your soul, and with all your mind. This is the greatest and first commandment. And a second is like it: You shall love your neighbor as yourself" (Matthew 22:37-39). Thus, the church's universal mission is one of love, and this love is to be directed to the whole world.

John Wesley, the founder of Methodism, referred to the concept of universality as the "catholic spirit". Wesley commented that "all (persons) will not see things alike. It is an unavoidable consequence of the present weakness and shortness of human understanding, that several (persons) will be of several minds in religion as well as in common life."[1]

Wesley believed that even though persons in the church might not always be in total agreement, we are still called to love God and our neighbors in the spirit of Christian love, justice and service.

In moving toward universality, we come to realize the synergistic effects of the Holy Spirit within the church, where the whole of the ministries becomes greater than the individual parts. Individuals and churches come to understand that they are players within the much broader scheme of God's divine will. God desires that we not only utilize our individual gifts, but our collective gifts to God's glory, as well.

The church is called to inculcate the reality that each of the smaller constituencies that comprise it (individuals, families, and other groups) are a part of a larger body - the family of God. An affirmation of the family of God might help churches resist the temptation to isolate and marginalize some of the groups with which it ministers.

At Ames United Methodist Church, it was important for us to understand the church's catholicity in terms that helped us to reach beyond the walls of the building and go into the community to engage in ministry. One means of accomplishing this was through the development of a membership care ministry. Through this ministry, members were invited to participate in making regular contacts with members and families who were either shut-in, or for other reasons not actively involved in the church's life. The results of the intentional efforts of the membership care ministry to be inclusive were evident in that many persons reported sensing an increased sense of connection and community within the church.

Another means by which universality was affirmed at Ames Church was through the work of the outreach ministry. This was particularly evident in the development of the church's addiction ministry in 1995. As discussed earlier, the development of this ministry was based on findings during a time of resident study at the Johns Hopkins Hospital Drug and Alcohol Treatment Facility. As a result of this experience, I concluded that it was important that we discern what God was calling us to do about the problems of substance abuse in our church and community.

This resulted in the Ames outreach ministry organizing an ecumenical gathering of persons from churches throughout the community, and the subsequent proposal to initiate a Christ-centered, Scripture-based twelve-step program we called "Christians in Recovery." (see Appendix 2)

Each church represented at the meeting agreed to support the addiction ministry through: (1) their prayers, (2) by holding "Christians in Recovery" meetings at their churches on various nights, and (3) by opening their doors to persons in the community who were dealing with addiction.

The results were seen in that many persons in the church and community became more willing to share about the addictions to drugs and alcohol with which they were dealing, and to seek help and support in overcoming their problems. As a direct result of the confidential nature of "Christians in

Recovery," it became apparent that many individuals and families within the church were searching for ways to overcome problems with substance abuse. As a means of addressing the more systemic concerns relative to substance abuse, the church now has a vision to open a full-service Christian Counseling Center to serve persons and families of the church and community who are looking to overcome their addictions.

Essential to congregational life and growth - and the development of inclusive community - is that each person be affirmed for the important gifts they possess. In offering their time, talent, treasures, as well as enthusiasm to the life of the church, they indelibly change the face and atmosphere of faith communities. Persons can be best integrated into the body of Christ, and sense their place as a part of the universal church by relating with other persons within the church who have authentic Christian faith, who are growing in that faith, who care about others, who are willing to diligently study the Scriptures, whose skills are both developed and are developing, and who are willing to serve faithfully in their communities. This is critical for the development of vital family ministry within African American churches.

§ § §

ENDNOTES

1. Albert Outler, *Theology in the Wesleyan Spirit* (Nashville; Discipleship resources, 1974), Outler develops the concept of Wesley's views on the "Catholic Spirit" at various points throughout the book.

CHAPTER EIGHT

PRINCIPLE FOUR: Apostolicity

The Black Church Should Develop The Means To Pass Its Faith and Traditions From One Generation To The Next

The Christian church is perpetuated by its traditions which derive primarily out of the witness of Christ in his life and ministry, and subsequently out of the establishment of the church as the instrument for the continuation of God's mission. Christian traditions have been passed from age to age, and largely comprise what the faith community has come to affirm as a system of beliefs and values.

In its apostolicity, the church affirms that its theological task does not start anew in each age or with each person. Christianity does not leap from the New Testament time into the present as though there is nothing to be learned from the people and events in between. Indeed there is a great deal to be learned from history, and from the joys and struggles of our faithful forbearers.

Authentic Christian faith is that which was passed down from the apostles - those men who were selected by Christ himself, and who personally witnessed and participated in the preaching, teaching, and healing ministries of the Lord. This same faith was passed from the apostles to the apostolic fathers who knew the apostles firsthand, and were thus heirs to the ministry of Christ. As the apostolic fathers received the faith and teachings of Christ directly from the apostles, this same faith was passed along to the church fathers. It is through the perpetuation of this lineage that we espouse belief in an authentic and historical Christian faith.

The transmission of the Christian faith among persons of widely varying backgrounds has constituted a dynamic element of Christian history, and bears witness to how the Holy Spirit has worked to bring the church to where it is today. The beliefs and practices that grew out of specific circumstances constitute the legacy of the corporate experience of earlier Christian communities.

It is in this context that we are reminded that the black church was not created in a vacuum. Thus, we understand that, in its contemporary context, it does not exist in a vacuum. The black church is called to recognize and steadfastly affirm its apostolicity and articulate how Christian traditions and African American culture have served to sustain it over the ages.

James Stallings, in *Telling the Story: Evangelism in the Black Churches*, reminds us of the importance of transmission of history and tradition in the black religious context. He points out that a healthy tradition is vital for the survival of a community. The pioneers of the black church movement in American passed on to their heirs a rich legacy.[1]

Perhaps the most profound, fundamental and powerful way that Christian apostolicity in the African American context can be seen is in the what Nicholas Cooper-Lewter and Henry Mitchell affirm as the family of God and humanity. It is widely recognized that the best way to acquire a healthy sense of equality and uniqueness is to grow up in a loving family. The difference is that (African Americans) define the family group in much broader terms. The larger vision of humankind as kinship group influences much of the interaction throughout the traditional Black community.

The black church has been one of the clearest manifestations of this notion of the extended family, and thus one of the progenitors of the beliefs and values extant in the black community.[2]

A temptation of the church in contemporary society - as it seeks to attract persons - may be to forsake many of the traditions that helped to form African American community over the ages. This temptation should be avoided as the church steadfastly seeks to evangelize contemporary cultures while continuing in its calling to maintain and build upon the rich history that has helped to shape and sustain the Christian faith community over the ages.

In recognizing its apostolicity, the church must see its link to the past, the value of that past, and how it will impact upon the future. The linkage between diverse cultures, how these cultures have been bound together in the past, and how the church is called to perpetuate apostolic witness and service to the world should also be recognized.

The apostle Paul was a Jew, Roman citizen, former persecutor of the Christian community, and one who would meet Jesus and become an apostle. Paul gives us a clear annunciation of the nature of the apostolic church when he proclaims, "For as many of you who have been baptized into Christ have put on Christ. There is neither Jew nor Greek, there is neither bond nor free, there is neither male nor female: for ye are all one in Christ Jesus" (Galatians 3:27-28).

Despite the growing diversity among people throughout our society, we are one in Christ - the One who historically has been "the Church's One foundation", and continues to unite the faith community in today's world.

At Ames United Methodist Church, developing constructive approaches to affirming our traditions, while also looking to address the contemporary needs in our midst in prophetic and visionary ways, became a particular area of focus. As a church steeped in tradition, the church found itself stagnating almost to the point of death.

We were reminded of the difference between tradition and traditionalism. While tradition can be defined as the living faith of the dead; traditionalism is the dead faith of the living.

While we affirmed tradition as an important value, it was important to move beyond traditionalism if we were going to fulfill God's vision for the church's future. Thus, in each ministry of the church - especially in worship- it became important to ask the often difficult question of why we did certain things. Was it because God had called us to do these things, or was it merely because of our traditionalism?

As we looked carefully at the distinction between tradition and traditionalism, we began to see as a congregation, ways that God was calling us to celebrate our traditions and culture, while at the same time moving boldly into the future in new and creative ways.

§ § §

ENDNOTES

1. James O. Stallings, *Telling the Story: Evangelism in the Black Churches* (Valley Forge, PA: Judson Press, 1988), p. 77.

2. Nicholas Cooper-Lewter and Henry Mitchell, *Soul Theology: The Heart of American Black Culture* (Nashville: Abingdon Press, 1986), p. 128.

CHAPTER NINE

PRINCIPLE FIVE: Kerygma

Worship Must Be At The Center Of
The Black Church's Life and Growth

Worship is at the heart of the experience of the black church. Zan Holmes, the pastor of St. Lukes United Methodist Church in Dallas, Texas goes so far as to postulate, "Show me a vital congregation and I will point you to a church that gives faithful attention to its worship."[1]

Churches often don't grow because their worship services are dry, lifeless, devoid of the passion and enthusiasm for the celebration of life that the Holy Spirit creates.[2]

Tyrone Gordon, the pastor of St. Mark United Methodist Church in Wichita, Kansas elaborates on this matter of the centrality of worship in the African American church experience. Praise and worship is the very heartbeat of the ministry of Saint Mark UMC. Whatever the ministry - be it youth, singles, or African American males; be it the ministry of racial reconciliation; be it helping persons become and stay addiction free; be it economic empowerment - its life, power, and meaning come from praise and worship.[3]

Black worship is the experience where the ritual dramas of freedom are actualized in the African American church. Black worship is more than praising and celebrating God and "how I got over." It is the theatre or forum wherein the dreams, ritual dramas, aspirations, and affirmation of freedom for black souls and spirits are actualized in a corporate context.[4]

To worship is to experience the reality of God, to touch Life. It is to know, to feel, to experience the resurrected Christ in the midst of the gathered community.

The word for worship is used in the Bible in some form or another no fewer than two hundred times. More than twenty times, the people of God are explicitly instructed to "worship the Lord." The word worship is derived from the Anglo-Saxon 'weorthscipe' which evolved into worthship and finally into the present word. The study of worship has been formally listed as the science of liturgies, or a study of the development of form in worship. The Greek word in the Septuagint, leitourgia, which translates the Hebrew word Aboda, is the basis for the word liturgy. In the New Testament the word leitourgia indicates the general service which Christians give unto God. It is literally "the work of the people."

Kerygma - or public expressions of the Christian faith - has been and continues to be critical to the development of faith in Christ. In the New Testament, one of the primary means by which Christian community grew was through public worship among themselves and with outsiders.

African American congregations generally agree that corporate Christian worship is acknowledgement of and response to the presence and power of God as revealed in Jesus the Christ through the work of the Holy Spirit. Descriptive words often heard in response to the question of one's understanding of worship include praise, adoration, reverence, thanksgiving, gratitude, celebration, penitence, submission, and commitment.[5]

William Temple offers the following thought on worship:

> To worship is to quicken the conscience by the holiness of God, to feed the mind with the truth of God, to purge the imagination by the beauty of God, to open the heart to the love of God, to devote the will to the purpose of God.[6]

Many persons are searching for images of God which are relevant to their life, culture and experience. These images often differ - and may even be in conflict with traditional images embraced by others. In their hesitancy to acquiesce and accept traditional concepts of the divine, and through their constant questioning and reflection, many persons today may arrive at different conclusions as to God's identity and purpose for their lives.

As in the past, persons are often seeking to actualize and experience God on a personal level. In the African American context, the search for images and experiences of God which are culturally relevant are critical to the appropriation of expressions of faith which are wholistic and lead persons and families along the path toward spiritual growth.

The worship celebration is generally considered to hold centrality as the focal point of Christian religious life. Opportunities to sing in choirs, to develop and present liturgies and prayers, as well as to share and proclaim the gospel of Jesus Christ offer congregants chances to creatively experience and participate in the true nature of worship.

Each aspect of the worship experience should speak in some way to the experiences, concerns, and needs of congregants, and those particular matters with which families are dealing. Through liturgies, proclamation, singing, the sacraments, and ordinances, leaders in African American congregations should ensure that worship incorporates various aspects of African American life and culture.

It is important that black churches remain sensitive to the realities extant in African American communities. This should be accomplished, however, while avoiding the temptation to accommodate and distort the true essence of the gospel of Jesus Christ, and its relevance in changing lives.

The sermon remains the center of the worship experience. Word and worship belong indissolubly to each other. All worship is an intelligent and loving response to the revelation of God, because it is the adoration of God's Name. Therefore acceptable worship is impossible without preaching. For preaching is making known the Name of the Lord, and worship is praising the name made known. Far from being an alien intrusion into worship, the reading and preaching of the Word are actually indispensable to it. The two cannot be divorced. Indeed it is their unnatural divorce which accounts for the low level of so much contemporary worship. Our worship is poor because our knowledge of God is poor, and our knowledge of God is poor because our preaching is poor. But when the Word of God is expounded in its fullness, and the congregation begins to glimpse the glory of the living God, they bow down in solemn awe and joyful wonder before (God's) throne.[7]

Carlyle Fielding Stewart III, the author *of Joy Songs, Trumpet Blasts, and Hallelujah Shouts*, and the pastor of Hope United Methodist Church in Southfield, Michigan which has experienced significant growth and vital witness in the black community, affirms the criticality of the sermon in helping persons experience a connection with God and with the church. Stewart asserts that the sermon in the African American context essentially entails four components: (1) poetic recitation, (2) imaginative insight, (3) spiritual pharmacology, and (4) spiritual and social transformation.[8]

In the African American church today, the tenuous balance must be struck between traditional and contemporary expressions of worship. Careful and prayerful attention should be given to the varieties of musical, visual, and dramatic presentation, and poetic expression that can be used to enhance the worship experience.

At Ames Church, the focus of worship was on celebration. Worship was a celebration of the goodness of God, and all that God continued to do in our lives. The tone and atmosphere of worship as celebration was one of joyful triumph over all the trials of life. Variety was encouraged through the church's five choirs, its liturgical dance ministry and various other forms of contemporary and traditional practice.

Carlyle Fielding Stewart discusses the importance of celebration in African American worship. Celebrate means to "observe with ceremonies of respect, festivity or rejoicing. To extol and praise." Prophetic worship buoyantly celebrates life in all its manifestations and fullness; it displays the gifts of the Holy Spirit. It passionately witnesses to the glory, honor, mercy, love, joy, and peace of Jesus Christ. This celebration not only involves the expression of feeling within the context of worship, but offers sentiment which conveys meaning; it reaches out to others and creates a sense of belonging and sharing of common goals, values and aspirations.[9]

Stewart points to four movements in celebrative worship: (1) Inspiration - A celebrative worship experience should inspire people to move closer to Christ. (2) Valuation - Celebrative worship speaks to the values and priorities of a particular congregation. (3) Consecration - Celebrative worship involves a candid recognition of spiritual, psychological, existential, and ethical truth in the lives of the people of God. (4) Motivation - Celebrative worship motivates people to participate in those realities and processes which will effect a constructive transformation of their spiritual lives.[10]

In a celebrative African American worship environment, the effective use of music is essential. Music at Ames Church consisted of various forms of gospel, Negro spirituals, traditional and contemporary songs, and involved the use of electronic as well acoustic instrumentation.

There was a time when the only 'acceptable' forms of musical instrumentation within churches were organs and pianos. Instruments like guitars, wind instruments, and percussion perhaps would be appropriate for use at camp meetings, revivals, and other less formal gatherings. Today, however, it is not unusual to find a full array of musical instrumentation incorporated into the worship celebration as churches seek to be culturally relevant to the whole family of God.

The role of music, and the types that are used in Christian worship, is a controversial issue. This is an area that can easily divide a church. Some see contemporary music as deplorable, while others believe it is an acceptable and effective means of communicating to younger congregants, and the unchurched.

This issue is not new. Martin Luther and the Wesleys (Charles and John) wrote hymns to common tavern tunes - the contemporary music of their day. Isaac Watts, who wrote such long-standing favorites as "Joy to the World", "Alas and Did My Savior Bleed?", and "We're Marching to Zion," is now considered one of the greatest hymn writers in history.

Charles Tinley and Thomas Dorsey, considered to be two of the "fathers" of African American gospel music, also used tunes familiar in the secular world to spread the gospel message.

Each of them was highly criticized in their day for writing such "contemporary" and "worldly" tunes to convey the truths of the gospel. Some in the church refused to use their music. But in the contexts of the years in which they lived - they realized the importance of finding a means to communicate the gospel to the masses. Jesus said, "And I, if I be lifted up from the earth, I will draw all (persons) unto me" (John 12:32). It is the task of the church in contemporary society to discover fresh and innovative approaches to lifting up Jesus to the masses, in order that persons will be drawn to Christ, and African American families will be preserved.

THE RISE OF NEOPENTECOSTALISM

Many churches and denominations have come to realize that challenges like widespread unemployment, eroding family structures, the absence of affordable housing, crime, violence and drug abuse are problems that black churches cannot effectively address by continuing to operate with the modalities that may have worked in the past.

Facing a bewildering variety of economic and social needs, churches are beginning to pool resources and strategies, thus ending their traditional isolation. A recent report entitled "The Black Church in America," issued by the Lilly Endowment said a change is occurring among black denominations and congregations that traditionally have been reluctant to join forces and make change.[11]

Today, many African American churches are becoming more open to offering contemporary and upbeat styles of worship and wholistic forms of social ministry. Perhaps, this is one of the primary reasons for the recent rise of what has been termed 'Neopentecostal' churches among mainline African American congregations. Recent studies indicate that Neopentecostal churches are among some of the fastest growing African American congregations in the United States. Many identify with black Baptist, African Methodist Episcopal (AME) and Church of God in Christ (COGIC) denominations, while United Methodists are also among the ranks.

Neopentecostal churches seem to have a great deal in common with many indigenous Asian and Hispanic faith communities which also place an emphasis upon engaging contemporary culture, charismatic worship, the Word of God, and innovative community and family ministries.

Pastors of Neopentecostal congregations are typically highly educated with many having earned doctorate degrees in ministry, theology or other social disciplines. In a survey of fifty ministers in the Baltimore, MD - Washington, DC region, who could be identified as fitting into the broad description of Neopentecostals (based on worship style and types of ministry), it was discovered that more than 90 percent (48) reported having completed advanced education in theology/divinity at least at the master's degree level. More than 70 percent of those surveyed (38) had completed doctoral work in the areas of theology or ministry (Doctor of Ministry, Theology, or Philosophy). Additionally, more than half (31) of the ministers reported having completed professional or graduate studies in another discipline.[12]

Neopentecostal ministries usually combine highly 'spirited' preaching and singing - similar to that found in traditional Pentecostal, Holiness and

Charismatic churches - with sophisticated social, community and family ministries.

Many congregations have memberships that cross socio-economic lines. They can be found in urban as well as suburban communities, and attract many low-income persons primarily because of the wide array of ministries and services that may be typically available (such as day care, tutorial, after-school, and food assistance programs). Many middle-class persons join Neopentecostal congregations because of: (1) a desire to participate in what they consider authentically African American worship, (2) programs that are available for all family members, as well as (3) a desire to engage in ministry that is relevant in empowering the communities out of which many of them have come.

The keys to the recent growth of Neopentecostal churches seem to be their focus on the redemptive and transforming power of vital worship, their ability to address the contemporary spiritual and cultural needs within their communities, along with their willingness to address the material concerns of individuals and families in their midst.

§ § §

ENDNOTES

1. Zan W. Holmes, Jr. *Encountering Jesus* (Nashville: Abingdon Press, 1992), p. 31.

2. Carlyle Fielding Stewart, III., *African American Church Growth: 12 Principles for Prophetic Ministry* (Nashville: Abingdon Press, 1994), p. 56.

3. Tyrone Gordon, "Praise and Practice", *The Circuit Rider* (Nashville, TN: United Methodist Publishing House, March 1996), p. 7.

4. Carlyle Fielding Stewart, III., *Soul Survivors: An African-American Spirituality* (Louisville, KY: Westminster John Knox Press.

5. Melva Wilson Costen, *African American Christian Worship* (Nashville: Abingdon Press, 1993), p. 91.

6. William Temple, cited in Richard Foster, *Celebration of Discipline* (New York: Harper and Row, 1978), p. 138.

7. John R. W. Stott, *Between Two Worlds* (Grand Rapids, MI: Eerdmans Publishing, 1982), p. 51.

8. Carlyle Fielding Stewart III, *Joy Songs, Trumpet Blasts and Hallelujah Shouts* (Lima, Ohio: CSS Publishing, 1997), these principles are elaborated upon throughout the book.

9. Stewart. *African American Church Growth*, p. 56.

10. Ibid., p. 58-62.

11. Religious News Service, "Isolation on Way Out for Black Churches", *The Washington Post* (Washington, DC: The Washington Post, 3/21/92).

12. Survey conducted by the author, and results based on data compiled through interviewing pastors/staff of churches in the Baltimore-Washington, DC region.

CHAPTER TEN

PRINCIPLE SIX: Diakonia

Ministry Should Offer Opportunities For Discipleship Through Service in the Church and Outreach With the Broader Community

The church's participation in the world can be translated as its mission. This mission is embodied in the mission of God (missio dei) and originates out of divine grace which is ultimately witnessed to by God's unconditional love in sending Jesus into the world. It is this mission that is the rationale and motivation for the church's participation in ministry with the world.

Dorothee Solle suggests that diakonia means serving or service. Christian service entails offering help for people in need, involvement in social and political processes - particularly in addressing oppressive structures of the church and society, as well as the ministries of sharing, healing and reconciliation. The church is the community of those who are there not to rule, but to serve.[1]

Service was a fundamental attribute of the early church, and has its foundation in the actions of Jesus who came to serve his own (Luke 12:37). This attitude of service is vividly seen in the act of Jesus washing the feet of his disciples (John 13:1-20). In the gospel account we are told, "And during supper Jesus, knowing that the Father had given all things into his hands, and that he had come from God and was going to God, got up from the table, took off his outer robe, and tied a towel around himself. Then he poured water into a basin and began to wash the disciples' feet and to wipe them with the towel that was tied around him" (John 13:2b-5).

This episode was occasioned by the contention among the disciples as to which of them would inherit the chief offices in the kingdom. It seems that the disciples had been "jockeying for position" in the kingdom. Jesus finally performed this humble act of foot-washing to help the disciples see that they had been called not to be served, but to serve.

The church's call is for its disciples to be servant-leaders. It is in our servanthood that we model the humility of Christ. In this sense, service involves not merely the good deed in and of itself, but it is self-offering and submission of our lives to Christ.

The teachings and actions of Jesus might lead today's church into a "radical re-imagination" of the possibilities for ministering with families. As Christ spoke to the rich young man and challenged him to look at his life, and the material wealth that he had attained from a new perspective - through a different set of lenses (Mark 10:17-22) - we are likewise called to constantly and introspectively re-evaluate and re-form our priorities and values in seeking to serve.

Here, Christ addressed this young man's question as to what is required for entrance into the kingdom of God. Christ shared with him three distinctive actions that are required for Christian discipleship. First, the young man was required to sell what he owned. Second, he had to give to the poor. And finally, he was required to follow Jesus.

As a similar reformation and re-orientation of values is shared with and experienced in the contemporary African American church, we come to the realization that God's grace has been, is now, and will continue to be the means by which each of us experiences the true manifestation of God in our lives.

This perspective may help churches view ministry differently. In order to fully utilize its resources and help preserve African American families, the church should engage in ministries which provide service within and outside its walls.

For instance, African American churches might develop outreach ministries and make regular visitations to homeless shelters, hospitals, prisons, or other institutions. Church members might also be encouraged to become involved with ecumenical and cooperative ministries which serve the community.

One way in which Ames United Methodist Church was able to serve persons in the church and the broader community was through the development - in 1995 - of a ten-week summer enrichment program for middle school aged youth. The program was called "Character Counts," was a collaborative effort supported by the church, the regional branch of the YMCA, and the Department of Juvenile Services of Harford County,

Maryland. A major objective of the program was to serve "at-risk" children who were referred by churches, government agencies and community groups. Many of these were youth who might not have had any other constructive supervision during the summer months.

"Character Counts" focused on the goals of helping the youth in the areas of: (1) leadership development, (2) team work, and (3) giving thought to future academic and career achievement. Regular recreational activities - including swimming, sports and visits to historical and amusement sites were an integral part of the program.

Paul said to the church at Ephesus, "I, therefore, the prisoner in the Lord, beg you to lead a life worthy of the calling to which you have been called, with all humility and gentleness, with patience, bearing with one another in love, making every effort to maintain the unity of the spirit in the bond of peace" (Ephesians 4:1-3). It is through our service and stewardship that we maintain the "unity of the spirit which is the bond of peace", as given to us by God.

As a part of the church's vision for serving families, each of the ministries at Ames Church was encouraged to develop a plan for regularly engaging in some form of service both within the church and in the broader community. The focus on service became central to the church's mission and vision, and critical to the discipleship and development of persons for increased responsibilities within the church.

Over time, we began to see the number of vital ministries in the church increase to over twenty five, with more people involved in Christian service.

§ § §

ENDNOTES

1. Dorothee Solle, *Thinking About God* (Philadelphia: Trinity Press, 1990), p. 141.

CHAPTER ELEVEN

PRINCIPLE SEVEN: Koinonia

Ministry Should Offer Opportunities For Fellowship Among Church Members and the Broader Community

Living in love and harmony with our neighbors is a central tenet of the teachings of Jesus Christ. Dr. Martin Luther King, Jr. stated that "Love is the most durable power in the world. This creative force, so beautifully exemplified in the life of our Christ, is the most potent instrument in (humanity's) quest for peace and security."[1]

As it has already been alluded to, in the Great Commandment, Jesus pointed out that in order for us to fully love God, we must develop loving, harmonious, caring, nurturing relationships with one another.

Author Marjorie Thompson speaks of the need to practice hospitality with one another through acts of compassion and community-building:

> Our love for one another is a direct expression of our love for God. "Those who do not love their brother or sister whom they have seen, cannot love God whom they have not seen." (1 John 4:20) One of our more persistent problems is that we do not see each other as sisters or brothers, much less love each other as such.[2]

In the early church, fellowship and a sense of community were exemplified in the sharing of not only social and spiritual gifts, but also in sharing material blessings. Therefore, none within the community of faith had need as long as persons had material resources to share (Acts 2:44-45). When the three thousand pilgrims who had been converted on the day of Pentecost remained in Jerusalem to be taught and established in the Christian faith, it was the church in Jerusalem that accepted responsibility for them (Acts 2:42-47). Many sold what they had and gave the proceeds for the support of these new believers.

Paul wrote to the Romans, "Be devoted to one another in brotherly love" (Romans 12:10). The word translated love here is not the greek word 'agape', the expression of volitional love, but 'phileo', the kind of platonic/brotherly love that we might experience in the caring that we share with our neighbors.

There is a tremendous need among persons for loving relationships. There is a yearning for a sense of belonging and becoming active participants within faith communities. Our willingness to share our diverse religious, social, and cultural experiences with one another serves to enrich, empower and enlighten the community of faith in order that the church might become more effective.

The concept of encouragement is closely related to fellowship. Donald Bubna in *Encouraging People*, points out that encouragement is an important concept with strong biblical roots. When the apostle Paul commands Christians to "encourage one another" (1 Thessalonians 5:11), he used the Greek word 'parakaleo'. This word comes from the same root as 'parakletos', the word we translate "Paraclete", or "the Comforter", referring to the Holy Spirit. Many scholars translate the word parakaleo "comfort" and, in fact, the words 'comfort' and 'encourage' can be used interchangeably.[3]

In this sense, Christians in fellowship with one another are called to "come alongside and help" each other. As churches engage in ministries of caring and compassion, they must remain mindful of the pervasive dysfunction and brokenness experienced within many African American families. Certainly, societal pressures have had profound financial, emotional and social effects on many families. The level and quality of participation in ministry might vary depending upon the degree of wholeness or brokenness, function or dysfunction, unity or disunity found within particular family systems.

At Ames United Methodist Church, fellowship became an integral part of the congregation's life together. Through several congregational surveys and numerous conversations, it was discovered that persons had a desire to develop more profound relationships with each other. They simply felt a need to "get to know" others in the church - beyond Sunday morning worship celebrations.

The church's theme/motto was, "We Are the Friendly Church, Where Jesus Christ is Lord." We decided to use our theme as the basis for developing fellowship and building community. Several ministries and programs were

THE BLACK FAMILY 63

developed for the specific purpose of encouraging Christian fellowship, and affirming the church as the family of God.

These ministries and programs typically involved entire families and included annual picnics, Christmas parties, fashion shows, and church outings to various sporting and entertainment events. We were constantly reminded of God's desire that we engage in Christian fellowship, and we began to experience a sense of strengthened relationships throughout the church.

African American churches also can often benefit from cooperating with other relevant institutions - including schools, community organizations, as well as other churches - in efforts to empower families and communities. Such cooperation essentially creates a broader base for ministry, where there is the possibility for churches having a greater impact upon the social fabric of the community.

In encouraging fellowship, it is also important to be reminded of how African American families are organized. Often, the extended family has been the primary form of family organization among blacks. A focus on the extended family as a means of fellowship can serve African American congregations very powerfully, and be the impetus for spiritual formation and discipleship among individuals and families.

Christian fellowship essentially involves sharing in the joy that a life in Christ offers. Richard Foster, a renown scholar and writer in the area of spirituality, offers in *Celebration of Discipline* that celebration is at the heart, the very essence of Christ. Christ entered the world on a high note of jubilation; the angels cried out, "I bring you good news of great joy." He left the world handing down His joy to the disciples as He told them, "these things I have spoken to you that my joy may be in you and that your joy may be full ..." (1 John 15:11).[4]

The life of Jesus was a life of joy and celebration, even amidst the tremendous obstacles, temptations, and doubts he faced. It was a life of rejoicing even in the midst of the dreadful suffering he was called to endure.

One of the most important things that Christians have been called to do is to offer joy to a world that often seems devoid of joy. Joy is indeed an essential aspect of the Good News of Jesus Christ. The joy that we share is at the heart of the church's existence as a community of grace and fellowship.

Through the joy of Jesus Christ, persons can begin to envision alternatives and glimmers of hope, amidst the pervasive temptations and struggles, the violence and destruction, that have become so much a part of the experience of many African American families. The notion of the family of God is celebrated as persons come to envision and experience their connectedness with one another. The church becomes that community full of the liberating power of Christ, who came to love us all.

§ § §

ENDNOTES

1. Martin Luther King, Jr. *Strength to Love* (New York: Harper and Row, 1963), p. 49.

2. Marjorie Thompson, *Soul Feast: An Invitation to the Christian Spiritual Life* (Louisville, KY: Westminster John Knox Press, 1995), p. 127.

3. Djonald Bubna, *Encouraging People* (Wheaton, IL: Tyndale House Publishing, 1988), p. 17.

4. Richard Foster, *Celebration of Discipline* (New York: Harper and Row, 1978), p. 163.

CONCLUSION

The task of this project has been to construct, in an integrative and coherent manner, the foundations for a model for addressing the critical matter of the black church's role in preserving African American families. Seven principles have been developed which may be helpful to churches in designing Christian ministries directed toward preserving African American families.

Certainly, many factors remain, both in the church and society, that affect black churches as they seek to engage in wholistic ministry which will positively impact families and communities.

It is incumbent upon the church to become increasingly aware of the realities which positively and adversely influence Christian ministry. This awareness will serve to empower congregations as they seek to develop the most effective means of ministering within the context of the increasingly diverse and complex needs, concerns and interests of persons who are a part of our churches and communities.

Throughout this project, my love and concern for the Christian church has been profoundly affirmed. My passion is one which is directed toward helping to address the question of how the church -as we have moved into the 21st century - can minister and transform persons, families and communities in the increasingly complex world in which we live.

Admittedly, many of my questions as to the direction of the church remain unanswered, awaiting further prayer, and Biblical, theological and sociological reflection. Ultimately, the question remains for me, "What does God call the Church, as the body of the faithful, to be and to do as we move into the next millennium?"

My prayer is that this question may be answered by those called to serve and lead the Church in the years to come.

APPENDIX 1

QUALITY OF LIFE RETREATS: A Model For Ministry With Aids Sufferers

Quality of Life Retreats

for persons with HIV/AIDS

A special project in the Baltimore-Washington Conference of the United Methodist Church

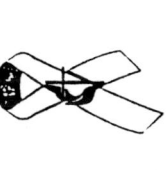

78 Church Road
Arnold, MD 21012-2314
410-974-1276

or

1729 Lamont Street, N.W.
Washington, DC 20010-2610
202-462-0234

Retreats are held in various locations:

Harper's Ferry
Washington, DC
Frederick

Usually scheduled in:
February
May
June
September
December

Separate retreats for

Adults

and

Parents and Children

Limited to 40 persons each retreat

Application fee: $10.00

Non-Refundable
(covers room, board and supplies)

Statement of Faith and Purpose

In affirmation of the love of God, this program is offered to all HIV-infected persons, regardless of religion, nationality, race, gender or sexual orientation.

We view the church as a healing instrument which can extend a caring, supportive ministry of prayer, education, advocacy and direct service.

The goal of our effort is to uphold and enhance the quality of individual life by nurturing hope, unconditional love, independence and self-determination.

Celebrate Life at a Quality of Life Retreat

The Quality of Life Retreat program began in 1988. Since then over forty retreats have been conducted.

The retreats are a connecting and coping experience for persons living with HIV/AIDS. It is a chance to get away, to get together, to interact and to learn the techniques and attitudes that are effective in dealing with the issues of long-term survival.

The retreats have four objectives:

1. To provide a safe, loving environment in which participants can be fully themselves, free of fears and inhibitions, and can deal openly with their deepest concerns.
2. To offer spiritual, practical, educational and health resources to those whose lives have been, are and will be affected personally by HIV infection.
3. To listen to what HIV infected persons have to say about their journeys.
4. To offer and develop a viable model of how the religious community can make a compassionate and effective response to this crisis.

Goals and Expectations

Our ultimate goal is to provide retreats that will be a connecting and coping experience for persons living with HIV/AIDS in the Baltimore/Washington metropolitan area as well as in the Hagerstown, MD, and Martinsburg, WV areas and all surrounding regions.

❧

Because of the intended diversity of participants at the retreats, we encourage community-building activities and emphasis on mutual respect and understanding.

❧

We want to include at least one HIV+ person in the planning of each retreat.

❧

We want to keep in mind that a broad-based, culturally-diverse group of planners and resource people can offer us the scope necessary for the best retreats.

❧

We want to avoid having resource people endorse their products, services, or methods of healing as the only route that can be taken, remembering that we are offering a range of options that needs to fit with each individual's own life path.

❧

We expect that the retreats will be alcohol and drug-free, except, of course, for prescribed medications.

❧

Because of allergies and fears, among other reasons, we request that participants and staff not bring pets on the retreats.

Information can be obtained by calling the telephone numbers listed on the front panel. All contributions are welcome and needed. Checks should be payable to "Quality of Life — Conference Treasurer" and sent to either address shown on the front.

APPENDIX 2

CHRISTIANS IN RECOVERY:
A Model For Church-based Addiction Ministry

APPENDIX

AMES UNITED METHODIST CHURCH

"CHRISTIAN'S RECOVERY GROUP"

"I can do all things through Christ which strengthened me."
-Philippians 4:13

PRAYER FOR SERENITY

"God, grant me the serenity to accept the

Things I cannot change,

Courage to change the things I can

And wisdom to know the difference;

Living one day at a time,

Enjoying one moment at a time;

Accepting hardship as a pathway to peace;

Taking, as Jesus did, this sinful world as it is,
not as I would have it;

Trusting that You will make all things right if I
surrender to Your will;

So that I may be reasonably happy in this life

And supremely happy with You forever in the
next."

AMEN.

Reinhold Niebuhr

Anonymity is the ... of our spiritual foundation, each of
us will protect the anonymity of all fellow members and
their families.

We welcome you to attend our meetings at:

Ames United Methodist Church
110 Baltimore Pike
Bel Air, Maryland

Friday evenings at 8:00 p.m.

Contact Persons:

Willie Walker, Crisis/Addiction's Counselor
(410) 879-8407

Rev. C. Anthony Hunt, Pastor of Ames UMC
(410) 838-0101

Debra Peaker, Program Coordinator
(410) 879-5482

Services at Ames UMC:

Sunday Church School/Bible Study....9 a.m.
Sunday Worship Service..............10:30 a.m.
Tuesday night Bible Study.................7 p.m.

The Pact

JAMES Recovery Group

We are Christians with a common handicap, that of being addicted to alcohol or drugs and other dependencies in their search for peace of mind.

Realizing that faith in Jesus Christ is the true way to peace, we are banded together in mutual effort to transfer dependence on alcohol to dependence on Jesus. We believe that what we cannot do alone, we can accomplish through helping one another.

What binds us together is the central ideal of our fellowship, that in sharing our strength with one another in humble strivings, Christ came, not to rule, but to serve, and taught that we should likewise be servants to one another.

Our common goal is to allow Jesus to become the guiding influence in our lives, and lead us to recovery.

Our Creed

I know that I cannot overcome alcohol/drug dependency by myself. I believe the healing power of Jesus Christ is available to help me. (Romans 3:23: "For all have sinned and fallen short of the glory of God.")

Because the presence of God is manifested through continued prayer, I will set aside two periods a day, morning, and evening, for communion with my Heavenly Father. I realize the need for daily Bible reading and use it to guide my daily living.

I recognize my need of Christian fellowship with Christians through the church of my choice. I know that in order to be victorious I must keep active in the service of Christ and His Church, and I will help others to victory.

I do not partake of any beverage containing alcohol. I know that it is the first drink that does the harm. Therefore, I do not drink.

I can be victorious because I know that God's strength is sufficient to supply all my needs.

12-Steps of A.A. and Biblical Comparisons

1. WE ADMITTED WE WERE POWERLESS OVER ALCOHOL, THAT OUR LIVES HAD BECOME UNMANAGEABLE. (Romans 7:18: "I know that nothing good lives in me, that is in my sinful nature. For I have the desire to do what is good, but I cannot carry it out.")

2. CAME TO BELIEVE: THAT A POWER GREATER THAN OURSELVES COULD RESTORE US TO SANITY. (II Corinthians 12:9 "...my grace is sufficient for you, for my power is made perfect in weakness." Romans 13:1: "Let every soul be subject unto the higher powers. For there is no power but of God.")

3. MADE A DECISION TO TURN OUR WILL AND OUR LIVES OVER TO THE CARE OF GOD AS WE UNDERSTOOD HIM. (Luke 9:23: "...if anyone would come after me, he must deny himself and take up his cross daily and follow me.")

4. MADE A SEARCHING AND FEARLESS MORAL INVENTORY OF OURSELVES. (Lamentations 3:40: "Let us examine our ways and test them, and let us return to the Lord.")

5. ADMITTED TO GOD, TO OURSELVES AND TO ANOTHER HUMAN BEING THE EXACT NATURE OF OUR WRONGS. (James 5:16: "Therefore confess your sins to each other and pray for each other so that you may be healed.")

6. WERE ENTIRELY READY TO HAVE GOD REMOVE ALL THESE DEFECTS OF CHARACTER. (ISAIAH 1:9: "If you are willing and obedient, you will eat the best from the land.")

7. HUMBLY ASKED HIM TO REMOVE OUR SHORTCOMINGS. (James 4:10: "Humble yourselves before the Lord, and he will lift you up.")

8. MADE A LIST OF ALL PERSONS WE HAD HARMED AND BECAME WILLING TO MAKE AMENDS TO THEM ALL. (Matthew 5:2324: "Therefore, if you are offering your gift at the altar, and there remember that your brother has something against you, leave your gift there in front of the altar. First go and be reconciled to your brother then come and offer your gift.")

9. MADE DIRECT AMENDS TO SUCH PEOPLE WHERE EVER POSSIBLE, EXCEPT WHEN TO DO SO WOULD INJURE THEM OR OTHERS. (Luke 6:38: "Give, and it will be given unto you. A good measure, pressed down, shaken together and running over, will be poured into your lap. For with the measure you use, it will be measured unto you.")

10. CONTINUED TO TAKE PERSONAL INVENTORY AND WHEN WE WERE WRONG, PROMPTLY ADMITTED IT. (Romans 12:3: "For by the grace given me I say to every one of youdo not think of yourself more highly than you ought, but rather think of yourself with sober judgment, in accordance with the measure of faith God has given you.")

11. SOUGHT THROUGH PRAYER AND MEDITATION TO IMPROVE OUR CONSCIOUS CONTACT WITH GOD AS WE UNDERSTOOD HIM, PRAYING ONLY FOR KNOWLEDGE OF HIS WILL FOR US AND THE POWER TO CARRY THAT OUT. (Psalm 19:14: "May the words of my mouth and the meditation of my heart be pleasing in your sight, O Lord, my rock and redeemer.")

12. HAVING HAD A SPIRITUAL AWAKENING AS THE RESULT OF THESE STEPS, WE TRIED TO CARRY THIS MESSAGE TO ALCOHOLICS, AND PRACTICE THESE PRINCIPLES IN ALL OUR AFFAIRS. (Galatians 6:12: "Brothers, if someone is caught in a sin, you who are spiritual should restore him gently. But watch yourself, or you also may be tempted. Carry each other's burdens, and in this you will fulfill the Law of Christ.")

CHRISTIANS IN RECOVERY PROLOGUE

THE BIBLE is the greatest book on recovery ever written. In its pages, we watch as God sets out a plan for the recovery of his broken people and creation. We meet numerous individuals whose hurting lives are mended through the wisdom and power of God. We meet the God who is waiting with arms outstretched for all of us to turn back to him, seek after his ways, and recover the wonderful plan he has for us.

Many of us are just waking up to the fact that recovery is an essential part of life for everyone. It is the simple but challenging process of daily seeking God's will for our life instead of demanding to go our own way. It is allowing God to do for us what we cannot do for ourselves, while also taking the steps necessary to draw closer to our Creator and Redeemer. It is a process of allowing God to heal our wounded soul so we can help others in the process of healing. All of us need to take part in this process; it is an inherent part of being human.

Let us set out together on a journey toward healing and newfound strength. Not strength found within ourselves, but strength found through trusting God and allowing him to direct our decisions and plans. This journey will take us through the Twelve Steps and other materials designed to help us focus on the powerful provisions God offers for recovery.

The Life Recovery Bible

APPENDIX 3

THE AMES UNITED METHODIST CHURCH BROCHURE OF MINISTRIES INCLUDING VISION STATEMENT

APPENDIX

Ames United Methodist Church
110 Baltimore Pike
Bel Air, Maryland 21014

Rev. C. Anthony Hunt, Pastor
Church: (410) 838-0161   Home: 836-7344

Ames United Methodist Church is known as "the friendly church" because of the love, warmth and heartfelt greetings extended to our visitors, members and friends. We take this opportunity to welcome you and ask that you return regularly.

Ames United Methodist Church is located in the center of Bel Air and attracts persons by and long time dwellers in Harford County. There are fifteen ministries to accommodate your needs. Church Services begin each Sunday morning with Church School followed by congregational worship. Special afternoon services are extended throughout the year. Ames UMC has a full time pastor and six lay speakers. Come back and join us at your convenience.

Our Membership

Our membership continues to grow each Sunday and our ministries continue to expand. There are programs for all ages—children, youth, and adults and families. There is a place for you

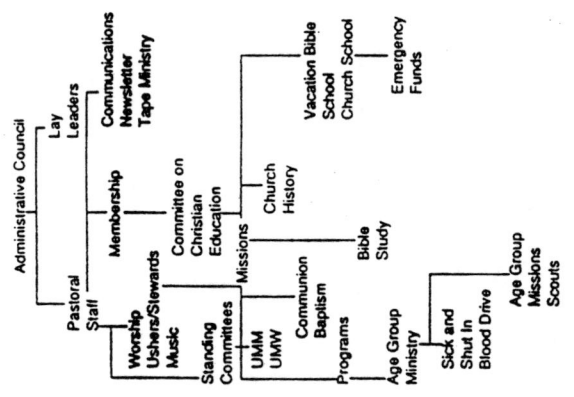

Lay Leadership

The purpose of lay leadership is to assist the minister in developing growth and understanding of the church's mission. The lay leaders also help the minister to bring spiritual inspiration and leadership to the congregation in the church and community.

For more information, please call the church office at (410) 838-0161 or the pastor at (410) 836-7344.

Organizational Chart

- Administrative Council
  - Pastoral Staff
  - Lay Leaders
    - Communications Newsletter Tape Ministry
  - Membership
    - Worship
    - Ushers/Stewards
    - Music
  - Committee on Christian Education
    - Church History
    - Vacation Bible School
    - Church School
    - Emergency Funds
  - Standing Committees
    - UMM
    - UMW
  - Missions
    - Communion
    - Baptism
    - Bible Study
    - Age Group Ministry
    - Sick and Shut In
    - Blood Drive
    - Age Group Missions
    - Scouts
  - Programs

A Foreword from our Pastor

We thank you for choosing to fellowship with Ames Church family today. You will find us to be a faith community that is filled with the love and joy of Jesus Christ. We offer many exciting worship and program activities during each week, and we invite you to involve yourself in any way that might be of interest. And if you are without a church home, we invite you to prayerfully consider making Ames your home.

Rev. Anthony Hunt

Ames United Methodist Church Mission Statement

We, the members of Ames United Methodist Church, are blessed and spirit led Christians. Our purpose is to know God through the ministries of worship, study, and service. By loving, praying, and evangelizing, we seek to touch the lives of our families, communities, and all God's people.

-Adopted at the 1993 Charge Conference

The Ames Church School

The church school implements the educational ministry of the church for all members including Sunday School each Sunday morning at 9:00 a.m. for all.

* Children and Youth ♦

This ministry provides programs for nurture, care, guidance and growth of children through the ages of 18.

♦ Adults ♦

This ministry provides programs for nurture, care, guidance and enrichment of adults. A bible class meets each Tuesday at 7:00 p.m. All are invited and encouraged to attend.

Church Council

This committee is responsible for establishing policy and for developing, coordinating and implementing programs for the church's mission. The committee consists of the following persons: The Minister; the Administrative Council President; the Lay Leader; the President of the United Methodist Women; the President of the United Methodist Men; the President of the Service Circle; the Superintendent of the Church School; Coordinators of age levels: children, youth and adults; the Trustees; the Committee on Finance; the Committee on Nominations; and the Pastor Parish Relations Committee.

United Methodist Men

This ministry of more than thirty men seeking to know Christ. They function with a governing body headed by a President, a Vice-President, Secretary, Treasurer and Chaplain. These dedicated individuals sponsor the church's Boy Scouts, participate in Sunday morning Adult Sunday School classes, attend Bible Study classes and sponsors an annual Men's Day Service. In addition to making sizable financial contributions to support the church, they organize recreational activities that include bowling, ball games and other family outings.

The United Methodist Women

The United Methodist Women are committed to serving God through the Methodist ministry. Each year, this group organizes programs, fellowship and service that involve the entire family. Support can also be seen in the groups sponsoring programs such as Call to Prayer and Self-Denial, World Day of Prayer, Women's Day, Homecoming and Black History Month

Boy Scouts

The Boy Scouts, ages 5-18 meet every Monday night except holidays. All are welcome.

Girl Scouts

If there is enough interest the group will be organized again.

Ushers

The Ushers have organized themselves and give service every Sunday to the church and congregation. The group sponsors many activities and welcome all others who are interested to join in their ministry.

The Prayer and Support Group

These groups welcome all who need and want prayer and support. Prayer and support groups meet at various times during the week.

Choirs

The Youth Choir provides an opportunity for the youth of the church to express themselves in song, ages 4-17.

The Senior Choir is made up of all and any interested members of the church older than 17 years to sing praises to the Lord.

The Karl Rodney Thomas (KRT) Inspirational Choir seeks to praise God in song with a selection of spiritual and gospel music. All ages are welcome.

APPENDIX 4

THE PRINCIPLES FOR THE CHURCH'S ROLE IN AFRICAN AMERICAN FAMILY PRESERVATION - SUCCINCTLY STATED

APPENDIX

PRINCIPLE ONE - UNITY
MINISTRY SHOULD BE INCLUSIVE IN ITS CONTEXT, AS THE ONENESS OF THE CHURCH IS AFFIRMED.

PRINCIPLE TWO - HOLINESS
MINISTRY SHOULD OFFER AN UNDERSTANDING OF THE CHURCH AS THE HOLY PEOPLE OF GOD.

PRINCIPLE THREE - CATHOLICITY (UNIVERSALITY)
MINISTRY SHOULD BE UNIVERSAL IN ITS CONTEXT AND SCOPE.

PRINCIPLE FOUR - APOSTOLICITY
THE BLACK CHURCH SHOULD DEVELOP THE MEANS TO PASS ITS FAITH AND TRADITIONS FROM ONE GENERATION TO THE NEXT.

PRINCIPLE FIVE - KERYGMA (PROCLAMATION/WORSHIP)
WORSHIP MUST BE AT THE CENTER OF THE BLACK CHURCH'S LIFE AND GROWTH.

PRINCIPLE SIX - DIAKONIA (SERVICE)
MINISTRY SHOULD OFFER OPPORTUNITIES FOR DISCIPLESHIP THROUGH SERVICE IN THE CHURCH AND OUTREACH WITH THE BROADER COMMUNITY.

PRINCIPLE SEVEN - KOINONIA (FELLOWSHIP)
MINISTRY SHOULD OFFER OPPORTUNITIES FOR FELLOWSHIP AMONG CHURCH MEMBERS AND THE BROADER COMMUNITY.

BIBLIOGRAPHY

Bakken, Kenneth L. *The Call to Wholeness: Health as a Spiritual Journey.* New York: Crossroad, 1992.

Bakken, Kenneth L. and Kathleen H. Hofeller. *The Journey Toward Wholeness: A Christ-centered Approach to Health and Healing.* New York: Crossroad, 1992.

Baldwin, Lewis V. and Horace L. Wallace. *Touched By Grace: Black Methodist Heritage in the United Methodist Church.* Nashville: Graded Press, 1986.

Billingsley, Andrew. *Climbing Jacob's Ladder: The Enduring Legacy of African-American Families.* New York: Simon and Schuster, 1992.

Bubna, Donald. *Encouraging People.* Wheaton, Il; Tyndale House Publishers, 1988.

Caldwell, Gilbert H. *Race, Racism, and Reconciliation.* Philadelphia: Simon Printing and Publishing, 1989.

Carter, Norvella and Matthew Parker, eds. *Women to Women: Perspectives of Fifteen African-American Christian Women.* Grand Rapids: Zondervan Publishing, 1996.

Circuit Rider. Nashville: United Methodist Publishing House, February, 1996; March, 1994.

Cone, James H. *For My People: Black Theology and the Black Church.* Maryknoll, NY: Orbis Books, 1996.

Cone, James H. *A Black Theology of Liberation.* New York: Orbis Books, 1986.

Cone, James H. *God of the Oppressed.* San Francisco: Harper, 1975.

Cooper-Lewter, Nicholas, and Henry H. Mitchell, *Soul Theology: The Heart of Black Culture.* Nashville, TN: Abingdon Press, 1986.

Costen, Melva Wilson. *African American Christian Worship*. Nashville: Abingdon Press, 1993.

Crandall, Ron. *Turnaround Strategies for the Small Church*. Nashville: Abingdon Press, 1995.

Crockett, Joseph V. *Teaching Scriptures from an African-American Perspective*. Nashville: Discipleship Resources, 1991.

Dubois, W.E.B. DuBois. *The Souls of Black Folk*. Greenwich, CT: Fawcett Publishing, 1953.

Dungy, Robert E. *Dimensions of Spirituality in the Black Experience*. Nashville: Abingdon Press, 1992.

Dyson, Michael Eric. *Race Rules: Navigating the Color Line*. New York: Addison-Wesley Publishing Company, 1996.

Dyson, Michael Eric. *Between God and Gangsta Rap: Bearing Witness to Black Culture*. New York: Oxford University Press, 1996.

Felder, Cain Hope. *Troubling Biblical Waters: Race, Class and Family*. New York: Orbis Books, 1989.

Felder, Cain Hope, ed. *Stony the Road We Trod: African American Biblical Interpretation*. Minneapolis, MN: Fortress Press, 1991.

Forbes, James. *The Holy Spirit and Preaching*. Nashville: Abingdon Press, 1989.

Foster, Charles and Grant Shockley. *Working with Black Youth*. Nashville: Abingdon Press, 1989.

Foster, Richard. *Celebration of Discipline*. New York: Harper and Row, 1978.

Frankl, Viktor E. *Man's Search for Meaning*. New York: Washington Square Press, 1984.

Franklin, John Hope. *From Slavery to Freedom: A History of Negro Americans.* New York: Alfred A. Knopf, 1947.

Frazier, E. Franklin. *The Negro Church in America.* New York: Schocken Books, 1963.

Freedman, Samuel G. *Upon this Rock: The Miracle of a Black Church.* New York: Harper Perennial, 1993.

Gates, Henry Louis and Cornell West. *The Future of the Race.* New York: Alfred A. Knopf, 1996.

Goatley, David Emmanuel. *Were You There: Godforsakenness in Slave Religion.* Maryknoll, NY: Orbis Books, 1996.

Gaustad, Edwin S. *A Documentary History of Religion in America, Since 1865.* Grand Rapids, MI: Eardmans Publishing, 1993.

Gutierrez, Gustavo. *On Job: God-Talk and the Suffering of the Innocent.* Maryknoll, NY: Orbis Books, 1985.

Harris, James H. *Pastoral Theology: A Black Church Perspective.* Minneapolis, MN: Fortress Press, 1991.

Hicks, H. Beecher. *Preaching Through a Storm.* Grand Rapids, MI: Zondervan, 1988.

Holmes, Zan W. *Encountering Jesus.* Nashville: Abingdon Press, 1992.

Hooks, Bell. *Yearning: race, gender and cultural politics.* Boston: South End Press, 1990.

Hunt, C. Anthony, et.el. *Building Hope: New Church Development in the African American Community.* New York: General Board of Global Ministries, United Methodist Church, 1997.

The Holy Bible, KJV. Nashville: Thomas Nelson Publishing, 1977.

June, Lee N. and Matthew Parker, eds. *Men to Men: Perspectives of Sixteen African-American Chrisitan Men*. Grand Rapids: Zondervan Publishing, 1996.

June, Lee N., ed. *The Black Family: Past, Present and Future*. Grand Rapids, MI: Zondervan Publishing, 1991.

Kelling, George L. and Catherine M. Coles. *Fixing Broken Windows: Restoring Order and Reducing Crime in Our Communities*. New York; Simon and Schuster, 1996.

King, Martin Luther, Jr. *Where Do We Go Form Here: Chaos or Community*. New York: Harper and Row, 1967.

King, Martin Luther, Jr. *Strength to Love*. New York: Harper and Row, 1963.

Kubler-Ross, Elisabeth. *AIDS: The Ultimate Challenge*. New York: MacMillan Publishing Co., 1987.

Kubler-Ross, Elisabeth. *On Death and Dying: What the Dying Have to Teach Doctors, Nurses, Clergy and Their Families*. New York: MacMillan Publishing Co., 1969.

Kunjufu, Jawanza. *Adam! Where are You? Why Most Black Men Don't Go to Church*. African American Images, 1994.

Lebacqz, Karen. *Justice in an Unjust World*. Minneapolis: Augsburg Publishing House, 1987.

Levert, Suzanne. *AIDS: In Search of a Killer*. New York: Julian Messner, 1987.

Lincoln, C. Eric. *The Black Church Since Frazier*. New York: Schocken Books, 1974.

Lincoln, C. Eric, and Mamiya, Lawrence H. *The Black Church in the African American Experience*. Durham, NC: Duke University Press, 1990.

BIBLIOGRAPHY 89

May, Gerald. *Simply Sane: The Spirituality of Mental Health.* New York: Crossroad, 1994.

McCaleb, George. *Faithful Over a Few Things.* Lithonia, GA: Orman Press, 1996.

McClain, William B. *Come Sunday: The Liturgy of Zion.* Nashville: Abingdon Press., 1990.

McClain, William B. *Black People in the Methodist Church.* Nashville: Abingdon Press., 1984.

McCray, Walter Arthur. *Black Young Adults: How to Reach Them, What to Teach Them.* Chicago: Black Light Fellowship, 1992.

Metzger, Bruce M. and Michael D. Coogan. *The Oxford Companion to the Bible* (NRSV). New York: Oxford University Press, 1993.

Metzger, Bruce M. and Roland E. Murphy. *The New Oxford Annotated Bible.* New York: Oxford University Press, 1991.

Military Chaplains' Review, Spring 1988: Care of HIV/AIDS Patients. Washington, DC: US Army Chaplaincy Services Support Agency, 1988.

National Conference of Catholic Bishops. *Economic Justice for All.* Washington, DC: National Conference of Catholic Bishops, 1986.

Osaigbovo, Rebecca Florence. *Chosen Vessels: Women of Color, Keys to Change,* Detroit, MI: DaBaR Services, 1992.

Outler, Albert C. *Theology in the Wesleyan Spirit.* Nashville, TN: Discipleship Resources, 1974.

Paris, Peter J. *The Social Teaching of the Black Churches.* Philadelphia, PA: Fortress Press, 1985.

Patterson, Sheron C. *Ministry with Single Black Adults.* Nashville: Discipleship Resources, 1995.

Pleasure, Mose, Jr. and Fred C. Lofton. *Living in Hell: The Dilemma of African American Survival.* Grand Rapids: Zondervan, 1995.

Reed, Gregory J. *Economic Empowerment Through the Church: A Blueprint for Progressive Community Development.* Grand Rapids: Zondervan, 1994.

Reid, Frank M. III. *The Nehemiah Plan: Preparing the Church to Rebuild Broken Lives.* Shippenburg, PA: Treasure House, 1993.

Richardson, Willie. *Reclaiming the Urban Family.* Grand Rapids, MI: Zondervan Publishing, 1996.

Schaller, Lyle E. *The Seven Day A Week Church.* Nashville: Abingdon Press, 1992.

Smith, Sid. *Reaching the Black Community Through the Sunday School.* Nashville: Convention Press, 1984.

Smith, Wallace Charles. *The Church in the Life of the Black Family.* Valley Forge, PA: Judson Press, 1985.

Snow, John. *Mortal Fear: Meditations on Death and AIDS.* Cambridge, MA: Cowley Publications, 1987.

Solle, Dorothee. *Thinking About God: An Introduction to Theology.* Philadelphia: Trinity Press International, 1990.

Spencer, Jon Michael. *Protest and Praise: Sacred Music of Black Religion.* Minneapolis: Fortress Press, 1990.

Stallings, James O. *Telling the Story; Evangelism in Black Churches.* Valley Forge: Judson Press, 1988.

Stewart, Carlyle Fielding. *Soul Survivors: An African American Spirituality.* Louisville, KY: Westminster Press, 1997.

Stewart, Carlyle Fielding. *Joy Songs, Trumpet Blasts, and Hallelujah Shouts: Sermons in the African-American Preaching Tradition.* Lima, OH: CSS Publishing, 1997.

Stewart, Carlyle Fielding. *Street Corner Theology: Indigenous Reflections on the Reality of God in the African American Experience.* Nashville, TN: James Winston Publishing, 1996.

Stewart, Carlyle Fielding. *African American Church Growth: 12 Principles for Prophetic Ministry.* Nashville: Abingdon Press, 1994.

Stott, John R. W. *Between Two Worlds.* Grand Rapids, MI: Eerdmans Publishing, 1982.

Walker, Clarence. *Breaking Strongholds in the African American Family.* Grand Rapids, MI: Zondervan Press, 1996.

Walker, Clarence. *Biblical Counseling with African Americans.* Grand Rapids, MI: Zondervan, 1991.

Washington, James Melvin. *Conversations with God.* New York: Harper Perennial, 1994.

Washington, Preston Robert. *God's Transforming Spirit: Black Church Renewal.* Valley Forge, PA: Judson Press, 1988.

Weems, Lovett. *Church Leadership.* Nashville: Abingdon Press, 1993.

Weems, Renita J. *Just a Sister Away: A Womanist Vision of Women's Relationships in the Bible.* Nashville: Innis Free Press, 1991.

West, Cornell. *Restoring Hope: Conversations on the Future of Black America.* Thornhall, ME: G.K. Hall and Co., 1997.

West, Cornel. *Prophetic Reflections: Notes on Race and Power in America.* Monroe, ME: Common Courage Press, 1997.

West, Cornel. *Race Matters.* Boston: Beacon Press, 1991.

West, Cornel. *Prophesy Deliverance!: An Afro-American Revolutionary Christianity.* Philadelphia, PA, Westminster Press, 1981.

Wimberly, Anne Streaty. *Soul Stories: African American Christian Education.* Nashville, TN: Abingdon Press, 1994.

Wimberly, Edward P. *African-American Pastoral Care.* Nashville, TN: Abingdon Press, 1991.

Wimberly, Edward P. *Prayer in Pastoral Counseling: Suffering, Healing and Discernment.* Louisville: Westminster/John Knox Press, 1990.

Wimberly, Edward P. *Pastoral Counseling in the Black Church.* Nashville: Abingdon Press, 1979.

Woodson, Carter G. *The History of the Negro Church*, Washington, DC: Associated Publishers, 1921.

ABOUT THE AUTHOR

C. Anthony Hunt is the Executive Director of the Multi-Ethnic Center of the United Methodist Church. A ordained minister, he is also currently a visiting lecturer and dean of the chapel at Goucher College, and has served in faculty and administrative positions at American University, McKendree College and Africa University (Zimbabwe), and has lectured extensively throughout the United States. Dr. Hunt is a graduate of the University of Maryland, Troy State University, and Wesley Theological Seminary, and earned his doctorate in theology at the Graduate Theological Foundation. He is the co-author of *Building Hope: New Church Development in the African American Community*, and has published numerous articles.